"This book is a convincing example of how contemporary psychoanalysis is constantly continuing and revitalizing the Freudian tradition of innovative interdisciplinary dialogues. Particularly severely traumatized analysands feel thrown out of time, never really having arrived in their own life, without a sense of past, present and future. The "search for lost times" (A la recherche du temps perdu, Proust) in psychoanalysis becomes an existential experience for many of them. However: how can such central psychic transformations be understood from the perspective of today's neurosciences, modern physics, philosophy and history? The outstanding authors of this volume take the reader on a stimulating journey towards a deeper understanding of time as one of the basic categories of human life."

Prof. Dr. Marianne Leuzinger-Bohleber, *Psychoanalytic principal investigator of the MODE Study, recipient of the IPA's Outstanding Scientific Achievement Award, 2023, Germany*

"An extraordinary collection that bridges psychoanalysis, neuroscience, and other sciences, like physics and history, to illuminate the multiple experiences of time. Profoundly relevant for understanding temporality in clinical practice and theory. A major contribution to contemporary psychoanalytic thought."

Dr. Jorge Eduardo Catelli, *Psy.D., Full Member and Training Analyst of the Argentine Psychoanalytic Association, Argentina*

"This volume is a fine literary achievement expressing the EPF spirit of dialogic exchange which arose in the Symposium on Time (2022). The chapters illustrate a creative crosspollination of inter-disciplinary thinking that evolved. The arguments are lively, compelling and generative. This book is sure to endure the test of time and become one of the classic EPF books."

Prof. Jan Abram, *EPF President (2024–2028) and author of* The Surviving Object: Psychoanalytic clinical essays on psychic survival-of-the-object (2022), *New Library of Psychoanalysis, Routledge, UK*

Time and the Experience of Time

With particular reference to neurobiology and neuroscience, this book explores a psychoanalytic understanding of time and how ideas of time affect our experiences in clinical practice and in everyday life.

The contributions examine new perspectives on numerous phenomena associated with the perception of time. In addition to the physics-based discussion of whether time and a now exist at all, whether the existence of time can be proven neuroscientifically, or how historical forms of the relationship to time develop, the authors consider memory, forgetting or regression, the emergence of the past in the present, and the anticipation of the future, as well as mental development and the psychoanalytical process, particularly from the aspect of presence. The book shows how psychoanalysis can escape scientific isolation and develop further in a lively, mutually enriching exchange with other sciences.

Drawing on scientific insights as well as the latest psychoanalytic thinking, this is essential reading for all psychoanalysts, psychotherapists, and anyone wanting a deeper understanding of the place of time in our lives.

Heribert Blass, Dr. med. (MD), is Training and Supervising Analyst for Adults, Children, and Adolescents; Specialist in Psychosomatic Medicine and Psychotherapy, Psychiatry, in Düsseldorf, Germany.

Leopoldo Bleger, Dr. med. (MD), is Supervisor Analyst of the French Association of Psychoanalysis (AFP), France.

Joëlle Picard, Dr. med. (MD), is Psychiatrist and Training Analyst (Supervisor) in Paris, France.

The New Library of Psychoanalysis 'Beyond the Couch' Series
General Editor: Alessandra Lemma

The New Library of Psychoanalysis was launched in 1987 in association with the Institute of Psychoanalysis, London. It aims to promote a widespread appreciation of psychoanalysis by supporting interdisciplinary dialogues with those working in the social sciences, the arts, medicine, psychology, psychotherapy, philosophy and with the general book-reading public.

The *Beyond the Couch* part of the series creates a forum dedicated to demonstrating this wider application of psychoanalytic ideas. These books, written primarily by psychoanalysts, specifically address the important contribution of psychoanalysis to contemporary intellectual, social and scientific debate.

Current members of the Advisory Board include Giovanna Di Ceglie, Liz Allison, Anne Patterson, Josh Cohen and Daniel Pick.

For a full list of all the titles in the New Library of Psychoanalysis main series and also the New Library of Psychoanalysis Teaching Series, please visit the Routledge website.

Titles in the 'Beyond The Couch' Series:

Hating, Abhorring and Wishing to Destroy: Psychoanalytic Essays on the Contemporary Moment
Edited By Donald Moss and Lynne Zeavin

Time and the Experience of Time: Psychoanalysis in Dialogue with History and Science
Edited by Heribert Blass, Leopoldo Bleger, and Joëlle Picard

For more information about this series, please visit: www.routledge.com/New-Library-of-Psychoanalysis-Beyond-the-Couch-Series/book-series/NLPBTC

Time and the Experience of Time

Psychoanalysis in Dialogue with History and Science

Edited by Heribert Blass, Leopoldo Bleger and Joëlle Picard

Routledge
Taylor & Francis Group

LONDON AND NEW YORK

Designed cover image: zmeel / Getty Images

First English edition published 2026
by Routledge
4 Park Square, Milton Park, Abingdon, Oxon, OX14 4RN

and by Routledge
605 Third Avenue, New York, NY 10158

*Routledge is an imprint of the Taylor & Francis Group, an informa
business*

First German edition published as *Zeit und Zeiterleben* by
Psychosozial-Verlag 2023

First English edition published by Routledge 2026

ISBN: 978-1-041-11468-0 (hbk)
ISBN: 978-1-041-11405-5 (pbk)
ISBN: 978-1-003-66011-8 (ebk)

DOI: 10.4324/9781003660118

Typeset in Times New Roman
by Apex CoVantage, LLC

In memory of Jorge Canestri (1942–2021)
EPF President 2016–2020

Contents

Contributors

Arnaldo Benini, Emeritus Professor of Neurosurgery at Zurich University. His books on neuroscientific subjects in Italian: *Che cosa sono io Il cervello alla ricerca di sé stesso* [What I am. The brain searching itself] 2009; *La coscienza imperfetta Le neuroscienze e il significato della vita* [Imperfect Consciousness and the Meaning of Life] 2012; *Neurobiologia del tempo* [Neurobiology of Time] 2017 second edition 2020; *La mente fragile Il Problema dell'Alzheimer* [The fragile mind. The Alzheimer Enigma] 2018. Essays in English are on Mieczyslaw Minkowski and his vision of aphasia in polyglots, on Vesalius, on Descartes', physiology of pain, on Domenico Cotugno and discovery of sciatic neuralgia, and on Oliver Sachs. Edition in Italian version of two books by K.R. Popper.

Charlotta Björklind lives in Stockholm and is a training and supervising analyst for adults, children, and adolescents. Member of the Swedish Psychoanalytical Association, working in private practice and as a senior lecturer at the Department of Psychology at Stockholm University. General Editor of the EPF and a member of the EPF executive 2016–2020 and, until recently, Director of Training of the Swedish Psychoanalytical Institute. Several publications on topics of sexuality and gender and on psychoanalysis in contemporary times and on the teaching of psychoanalysis.

Heribert Blass, Dr. med. (MD), training and supervising analyst for adults, children and adolescents; specialist in psychosomatic medicine and psychotherapy, psychiatry. Member of the German Psychoanalytical Association (DPV). Since August 2025, President of the International Psychoanalytical Association (IPA). 2020–2024 President of the European Psychoanalytical Federation (EPF). Working in private practice in

Düsseldorf, Germany. Several publications, amongst others on the psychic representation of the father, on male identity and sexuality, on aspects of gender and gender transformation, psychoanalytic supervision and clinical aspects of child, and adolescent analysis.

Leopoldo Bleger, Dr. med. (MD), lives in Paris since he left Argentina in 1976, where he trained as a doctor and psychiatrist. Full member (supervisor) of the French Psychoanalytical Association (APF), member of the EPF Working Party on "Specificity of psychoanalytic treatment today". EPF General Secretary 2012–2016, President of his society 2017–2019. Lately he has written "Some Remarks on the Formation of Psychoanalysts" (IPA podcast) and *Analyse en présence, analyse à distance*, 2024.

Katy Bogliatto, Dr. med. (MD), is a child psychiatrist, training analyst of the Belgian Psychoanalytical Society, and former treasurer of the European Psychoanalytical Federation (EPF) (2016–2020). Since August 2025, Vice President of the International Psychoanalytical Association (IPA). She works in private practice with adults, adolescents, children, parents, and their babies and is a consultant at the Assisted Reproduction Center of Chirec, Brussels. She teaches at the Free University of Brussels, third cycle on the "Certificate in Children & Adolescent Psychotherapeutic Clinic". She's member of the editorial board of the *Revue Belge de Psychanalyse*.

Jorge Canestri, Dr. med. (MD), was born in Buenos Aires in 1942 and died in Rome in 2021. He was a psychiatrist and psychoanalyst, and a training and supervising analyst for the Italian Psychoanalytical Association and for the Argentine Psychoanalytic Association. His psychoanalytical training took place in Buenos Aires; in 1976, he emigrated to Italy and lived and worked in Rome, where he also became Professor of Psychology of Mental Health at the Roma 3 University. He was very active in the International Psychoanalytic Association (IPA) and in the European Psychoanalytical Federation (EPF). He held various key positions within the IPA (Chair of Ethics Committee 2001–2005, IPA Global Representative for Europe 2005–2007, Chair of International New Groups Committee 2009–2013). He was Chair of the Working Party on Theoretical Issues of the EPF 2001–2006, and he was President of the EPF 2016–2020. He was a member of the editorial board of the *International Journal of Psychoanalysis* and was the Mary S. Sigourney Award recipient in 2004. He published numerous psychoanalytical papers in books and reviews and was co-author of *The Babel of the Unconscious. Mother Tongue and Foreign Languages in the Psychoanalytic Dimension*; Editor (with Marianne Leuzinger-Bohleber and Anna Ursula Dreher) of *Pluralism and Unity? Methods of research in psychoanalysis*; Editor of *Psychoanalysis: from practice to theory*. He was also Director of the webpage Psychoanalysis and logical mathematical thought.

François Hartog is a historian, Professor Emeritus, Ecole des hautes études en sciences sociales (Paris). He has published a dozen books, translated into several languages. His first book on time was *Régimes d'historicité, Présentisme et Expériences du temps – Regimes of Historicity, Presentism and Experiences of Time*. Last book translated into English: *Chronos, The West Confronts Time*, 2022.

Gernot Münster has been full Professor of Theoretical Physics and director of the Institute for Theoretical Physics at the University of Münster. He studied physics and mathematics at the universities of Kiel and Hamburg, where he obtained a PhD in theoretical physics before holding research and assistant positions at the Deutsches Elektronen-Synchrotron (DESY), Bern and Hamburg. His research focuses on the theory of elementary particles and statistical physics. He has held several academic offices, including member of the university senate, chairman of the Scientific Council of the John von Neumann Institute for Computing, and founding member and member of the Scientific Advisory Council of the Centre for Philosophy of Science.

Bernd Nissen, Dr. phil. (PhD), psychoanalyst and training analyst (DPV/IPA) in private practice. Main areas of work: Among other things, metapsychological, theoretical, and clinical conceptualisation of autistic and nameless states and reflections on "time" and "space" in psychic systems. Co-editor of the *Yearbook of Psychoanalysis*. Publications in numerous languages.

Joëlle Picard, Dr. med. (MD), lives in Paris, where she works in private practice. She is a psychiatrist and training analyst (supervisor). She is one of the founders of the SPRF, past President of the Psychoanalytic Society for Research and Training (SPRF) 2015–2019, former EPF Vice President

(2020–2024), and Chair of the EPF House from 2024. Her analytical interests focus on psychosomatic patients and young adults. She is also very interested in the relationship between the analytical field and related scientific fields, particularly history.

Jasminka Šuljagić is a training and supervising analyst of the Psychoanalytical Society of Serbia, previous president of this society, and a member of the executive committee of the EPF as General Editor (2020–2024). She works in private practice in Belgrade. Over the previous years, she has been engaged in various tasks within the EPF and IPA. Currently, she is chair of the EPF Archive Committee and of the Institutional Matters Forum, with a recently published book: *Dynamics of Psychoanalytic Institutions*. She has many presentations and publications in seven different languages.

Preface

We turn to an increasingly innovative multiplicity of devices to know clock time, but these days, we also recognise that there is no single definition of time itself, no unity in how we conceive of it.

Current research in neurobiology, for instance, reveals different rhythms and organisations of time right within the human being, apart from the well-known circadian rhythm. It's fascinating to consider that there seem to be different clocks in the brain and in other organs, all set differently. Time and body are intermingled – our body is subject to time, and death of the body is the end of personal time.

Physicists do not agree on one theory of time even within their own field – quantum theorists and proponents of relativity conceive of it differently; and relativity can even work perfectly well without any notion of time.

This book is anchored in psychoanalytic experiences and explorations of time.

Although psychoanalysis can lay no claim to the concept of time, many of its conceptualisations are concerned with it. Even within the precise parameters of the analytic session, we are confronted with different regimes of time: from the fixed clock time of 45 or 50 minutes on one hand to the "tempo" of the interpretation on the other. The a-temporality of the unconscious is always in the background while also reigning above all else. The time in the session offers the possibility to "re-signify" within that session itself – i.e. what is said now will have a different echo with another association later on – and allows the "Nachträglichkeit" or "après-coup" to operate. "Nachträglichkeit" (Freud, 1898a, G.W., p. 511), "après-coup" or the "retroactive resignification that assigns signification *a posteriori* to a 'previous traumatic fact'" (Glocer Fiorini & Canestri, 2009, p. xxvii, a better formulation than "deferred action" in the English Standard Edition, Vol. 3, p. 281) is also of significant importance in the psychoanalytic process: it opens up the opportunity to retroactively process the past in the present. Its variation, the diphasic psychic organisation, is a primary notion of time in psychoanalysis. And in this way, the present and the past intertwine paradoxically from two sides.

As it's a polysemous word, the definition of time seems difficult if not impossible.

This book invites you, dear reader, into the halls of a symposium held in Brussels in April 2022 by the European Psychoanalytic Federation (EPF) symposium, where we had gathered to understand the dimension of time from a psychoanalytic and neighbourhood science perspective. The COVID pandemic still lingered, and our meeting was hybrid – many arrived in person while others joined the discussions online. This book brings you the richness of the symposium through the printed word.

A scientific federation of 42 national psychoanalytic societies, and some from outside Europe for structural reasons, the EPF provided both the financial and organisational basis for the symposium and also the publication of this book.

Jorge Canestri, EPF president from 2016 through 2020, had been nursing in his mind the idea of such a symposium for several years, having co-edited a book entitled *The Experience of Time* (2009). In 2018, Canestri, Leopoldo Bleger, former general secretary; and Heribert Blass, then vice president, began thinking about the structure of such an interdisciplinary symposium. A change in the EPF board occurred in 2020 when Blass took office as new EPF president, and Joëlle Picard, as one of the two new vice presidents, joined Bleger on the organising committee.

Alas, in May 2021, we were greatly dismayed by the death of Jorge Canestri and deeply wished to dedicate the symposium to his memory, just as we wish to do with this book. An exchange of perspectives between specialists from different disciplines would broaden and clarify our thinking around time; such was Canestri's intention, and ours, in wishing to organise this symposium.

Alongside the topic of time, the interdisciplinary exchange was equally important. "Hard" sciences, in their claim for hegemony, assert that the study of the brain will explain psychic life. Some psychoanalysts consider neuroscience to be creating a new – or even "real" – foundation for psychoanalysis. Questions of methodology and epistemology are present almost all the time in the work of physicists and neuroscientists; and historiography, the history of approaches to historical methods, is a key area of work for historians – but in psychoanalysis, up to what point are we concerned with methodological and epistemological questions?

Canestri was convinced that only an openness to interdisciplinary exchange could keep psychoanalysis alive in the circle of sciences and wider society. In his 2009 book, he wrote, "As we said, our focus on the factor of time assumes that we take cognisance of the studies on time produced by other disciplines: physics, philosophy, and history. Thus, we learn that there is no one-dimensional interpretation of time" (2009, p. xxvi).

This spirit inspired and steered our planning of this symposium and enabled us to bring together outstanding scientists from across Europe: from Germany, Professor Gernot Münster, a physicist; Swiss-Italian Professor Arnaldo Benini, a neurosurgeon and neurologist; from France, Professor François Hartog, a historian; and again from Germany, Dr Bernd Nissen, a psychoanalyst. All four have addressed the topic of time within their own fields of expertise. Their keynote lectures were followed by a paper in response from a psychoanalyst. This volume contains the keynote lectures and the commentaries.

Leopoldo Bleger introduces the collection with his thoughts on the scientific position of psychoanalysis and his perspective on Canestri's interdisciplinary approach. Heribert Blass provides an overview encompassing the sciences brought together in this book – physics, neurobiology, history, and psychoanalysis. And as a posthumous tribute, we include Canestri's 2015 article, "The Complex Dialogue Between Neuroscience and Psychoanalysis"; it also displays the scientific quality of his psychoanalytic thinking. To conclude, we offer some "Afterthoughts on Time" that evolved from the papers and ensuing discussions.

Without such inspiring and collegial cooperation, scientific and praxeological development within psychoanalysis would not be possible.

Our sincere thanks go to Anne Patterson as Series Editor and the entire editorial team of the New Library of Psychoanalysis, in particular Sharadha Bain, who, with great commitment and skill, has made our manuscript more fluent, understandable, and readable for a wider readership.

Heribert Blass, Leopoldo Bleger, and Joëlle Picard

References

Freud, S. (1898a). Die Sexualität in der Ätiologie der Neurosen. *GW* 1, 491–516

Freud, S. (1898b). Sexuality in the Aetiology of the Neuroses. *SE* 3, 259–285

Glocer Fiorini, L. & Canestri. J. (eds). (2009). *The Experience of Time. Psychoanalytic Perspectives*. London and New York: Routledge

Chapter 1

On the EPF symposium on time April 9–10, 2022, and on the present book

Heribert Blass

Introduction

Why does the subject of time matter in psychoanalysis? It might not be immediately self-evident even to analysts, but a second look reveals how important the field of time is to our work. This was the theme of the EPF symposium on time in April 2022, and some fundamental aspects of this question will also be discussed in this book.

Back in 1971, Hans Loewald remarked that few psychoanalytic papers touched on the topic of time and the experience of it in beyond a merely marginal way, although there had been a recent increase in interest. In his book, *The Experience of Time,* he enumerates phenomena and concepts related to time that are of importance to us as psychoanalysts:

> memory, forgetting, regression, repetition, anticipation, presentation, representation; the influence of the past on the present in thought, feeling and behaviour; delay of gratification and action; sleep-wakefulness and other rhythmicities in mental life; variations and abnormalities in the subjective sense of elapsed time; the so-called timelessness of the id; the role of imagination and fantasy in structuring the future; values, standards and ideals future-oriented categories; concepts such as object constancy and self-identity; not to mention the important factor of time in the psychoanalytic situation itself, in technical aspect, appointments, length of hour etc.
>
> (1972, p. 402)

Nearly forty years later, André Green (2018 [2009]) noted that the problem of time was much less discussed among psychoanalysts than issues related to space. He spoke of an ignorance of time, which had led from

DOI: 10.4324/9781003660118-1

"a murder of time"[1] to a misrecognition of temporality in psychoanalysis. He pointed out (2003, p. 790) that Freud had spent more than forty years developing multiple hypotheses on the meaning of time featuring characteristic concepts. A complex theory of temporality emerged from this endeavour. At the end of Freud's investigations into time stood the idea of historical truth – something that Green described as unfortunately forgotten since. Since metapsychology was also considered obsolete and only the genetic point of view survived, Freud's concepts about time faded away.

Green saw Freud's hypotheses as still useful, only if differentiated according to mental functioning modes and different patient groups (2003, p. 790). He tried to recast Freud's organisation of psychic life into the following groups as a polychronic structure – drives, unconscious thoughts and fantasies, memory, conscious experience, and also the meaning of *nachträglich*[2] (après-coup in French; or "deferred action" as a not-quite-accurate translation in the Standard Edition). He conceived of this as "exploded time" – *temps éclaté* in French or *zersplitterte Zeit* in German.

He also differentiated between the vivid timelessness of the unconscious determined by Eros and a destructive fantasy of being able to stop the passage of time, which leads to the freezing of the experience of time and the "murder of time". This destructive imagination, which is directed against one's own psychic life, also destroys the temporal processes and experiences associated with the "time of the other" – i.e. the internal object, parental figures. It is important to note that Green opposed an exclusively psychological conception of time. Rather, for him, biological and psychic determinants are equally organisers of time.

Ardently advocating an interdisciplinary approach, Jorge Canestri emphasised that "'time is of the essence': it is something indispensable that we are compelled to respect" (Canestri & Glocer Fiorini, 2018 [2009], p. xxiii), but felt strongly that psychoanalytic discourse would be meaningful only if modifications brought by natural science to the understanding of time were not ignored.

Since the early twentieth century, developments within modern physics have significantly revised the previously naive understanding of time, and we have had to give up the idea of a single "absolute time" and "absolute space" (see G. Münster's chapter in this book). Aristotelian thinking assumed a preferred state of rest which anybody would take up if not driven by some force or impulse; however, Newton's laws have led to the realisation that there is no unique standard of rest (Hawking & Mlodinow, 2005, p. 22). The discovery of the speed of light and, subsequently, Einstein's theory of relativity led to the view that the laws of nature must be the same for all moving observers regardless of their speed, and this also applies to the speed of light.

Hawking and Mlodinow (2005, p. 29) give the example of a moving train in which ping-pong is being played. If a player hits the ball towards the front of the train at a speed of 10 kilometres per hour, a fictitious observer on the platform would be expected to determine the speed of the ball at 160 kilometres per hour – the 10 at which the ball is moving relative to the train plus the 150 at which the train is moving relative to the earth. What is the speed of the ball now: 10 or 160 kilometres per hour? There can be no unambiguous answer or no solution of an absolute speed. The speed can only be stated relative to the train or relative to the earth. According to the theory of relativity, each observer has his or her own measure of time, and clocks of the same construction do not necessarily have to agree in their indications with different observers.

Physics considers time to be the fourth dimension. Einstein's theory of relativity posits that time does not exist detached and independent of space with its three-dimensional coordinates of length, height and width but combines with space to form the entity of "space-time" (Hawking & Mlodinow, p. 35). Due to "curved space" and the flow of time, there is the "twin paradox": a pair of twins living at different altitudes would age differently. The twin who lives on a mountaintop would age faster than the twin residing at sea level, though the difference in age would be small. However, should one twin go for a long voyage in a spaceship which accelerated to nearly the speed of light, on return to Earth, he would be much younger than the twin who remained on earth.

For us as psychoanalysts, participant observers in our field, these developments in physics could raise question such as: Can we really find an "historical truth"? Or how do we deal with different views that arise from "inside" and "outside" of experiences between the two people in the consulting room? Physics also gives us Heisenberg's uncertainty principle, inviting us – and other disciplines too – to be humble.

Further, "real" time implies a distinct difference between going forward to the future or backwards to the past; only the past can be remembered, and the future exists only in fantasy. The unification, however, of gravity with quantum mechanics creates the notion of an "imaginary" time which is confused with direction in space. In imaginary time, forward or backward makes no difference; and for the law of physics, the distinction between past and future no longer exists when considering the fundamental operations between particles (cp. Canestri, xxiv).

Stephen Hawking even writes that in theory, time travel could be possible due to wormholes. At the end of this introduction, I will offer an example of 'time travel' within a psychoanalytic process.

Returning to physics, Hawking and Mlodinow describe how the Big Bang, estimated at about 13.7 billion years ago, is considered the beginning of time and that the "time arrow" now proceeds in the direction of ever greater disorder or entropy. They identify three time arrows: the thermodynamic arrow of entropy; the psychological arrow, as the brain too obeys the second law of thermodynamics; and the cosmological arrow which points to the fact that the universe expands and does not contract.

Psychoanalyst and former president of the International Psychoanalytical Association Charles Hanly, in his 2018 [2009] article, took the second law of thermodynamics and the fact that our brain is also subject to this law as the starting point for a complex inquiry. As the "subjective fluctuations in the sense of time are relative to the individual's moods and unconscious phantasies", and as in "nature, time is relative to the velocity of matter in motion" – "What, then, are we to make of Freud's often repeated idea of the timelessness of the unconscious?" (p. 24). Hanly's argument cannot be reproduced here in full, but he demonstrates convincingly that Freud's Lamarckian view, according to which ideational archaic heritages in the realm of sexual and aggressive drives "would have transgenerational genetic immortality dating from the origins of mankind" (p. 26), is scientifically untenable. This includes the Oedipus complex.

Hanly vividly shows that recourse to alleged transgenerational immortality and timelessness is not necessary for proof of a return of infantile aggressive drives in adulthood and reaction formations[3] directed against it. He writes:

> Unconscious processes are not themselves timeless, contrary to Freud's (1896s, 1920g) assertions that they are intrinsically timeless and that time does not apply to them. Unconscious contents originate with developmental or object relational calamities (usually both intertwined); they have a beginning; they will have a variable history according to their influence in the life of the individual and of the

individual's relational life on them; and they will end with death. In themselves, *unconscious processes are no less temporal than conscious processes*. It is just that they function differently, and one of the differences is that they are not, once established, easily subject to the influences of experience, development, and relations.

(p. 30/31; emphasis by HB)

Let's return to physics. How do we feel when we hear from theoretical physicist Carlo Rovelli (2019) that time does not exist? He refers to the end of the present, because "now" would mean nothing. As Einstein discovered, both mass and speed slow down time on two identical clocks. Time passes more slowly for a person on the move than for one who stays still.

The concept of "simultaneity" in Einstein's theory of relativity also challenges our intuitive idea of a shared "now". According to relativity, "now" depends on the observer's velocity and position. Therefore, when considering two different, distant locations – such as a point on earth and a point on planet Proxima B – "now" could be seen as either in the past or the future from the other's perspective, depending on their relative velocities. And in the universe, a massive black hole slows time to such a degree that at its border, time stands still (p. 49). Thus, the "present of the universe" does not exist. And of course, time is elastic within our personal experience of it.

Finally, after taking into account "the three fundamental discoveries of quantum mechanics (. . .): granularity, indeterminacy and the relational aspect of physical variables" that Rovelli says demolish "further the little that was left of our idea of time (p. 73), he invites us to "enter the world without time" (p. 81). He explains that after losing all assumed pieces of time – singularity, direction, independence, the present and continuity – the world remains a "network of *events*." Nothing *is*; things happen instead. This leads him to conceive of the world as being "in a ceaseless process of change" (p. 86). "The world is not a collection of things, it is a collection of events" (p. 87). *Things* persist in time, whereas *events* have a limited duration. We can ask ourselves where a thing like a stone will be tomorrow – even if the stone is, in reality, a complex vibration of quantum fields – but that's very different to asking where an event like a kiss will be tomorrow. "The world is made up of networks of kisses, not of stones" (p. 87). In essence, Rovelli concludes that the time variable is not required to describe the world.

For psychoanalysts who are engaged with processes of psychic change, this central passage from Rovelli is particularly noteworthy:

> There is no need in any of this to choose a privileged variable and call it "time". What we need, if we want to do science, is a theory that tells us how the variables change with respect to each other. That is to say, how one changes when others change. The fundamental theory of the world must be constructed in this way; it does not need a time variable: it needs to tell us only how the things that we see in the world vary with respect to each other. That is to say, what the relations may be between these variables.
>
> (p. 103)

When applying such ideas to the psychoanalytic process, psychoanalysts can readily agree with the idea of mutually changing variables, because psychological changes also occur in the psychoanalytic process through mutual emotional attunement between analyst and analysand. However, the idea of suspending time is more difficult to accept, especially since the immediate *presence* of the analyst is clinically significant (see Bernd Nissen's contribution in this volume).

Another physicist, Gernot Münster, a keynote speaker at the symposium, has already earlier (2010) and now in his contribution to this volume stated that, from a physical point of view, there is no such thing as 'now'. For him, the concept of time is theory-laden, and he too concludes that there is no uniform concept of simultaneity. But Münster draws on a distinction made by the philosopher McTaggart and speaks of events in an A-series with a reference to the past, present, and future, and a B-series in which only linear references, such as earlier or later, are possible. In this sense, he – but without explicitly stating this – does not agree with Rovelli's radical approach of wanting to abandon the concept of time altogether (see Gernot Münster's contribution to this volume).

Historian François Hartog, in his book *Chronos* (2020), wrote of retaining Rovelli's approach and also the background of his conceptual thinking. Hartog was a keynote speaker at the symposium, and his paper follows later in this book. However, the neuroscientist Arnaldo Benini, another speaker at the symposium and thereby a contributor to this book, avers that neuroscience has proven that a concept which sees time as real only insofar as there are things that change would not be true (2020, p. 22). He put forward studies in which time related to a fundamental dimension of the life of living beings with a nervous system. Based on analyses of a disturbed sense of time in patients with sometimes dramatic brain lesions, he states that for neuroscience, time is real.

Benini finds the inconsistency of today's natural sciences regrettable – that while for a quantum physicist, time is an "archaic, obsolete and deceptive mental construct", for a neuroscientist, it is "one of the realities closest to the heart; i.e. to the basic functions of nature" (2020, p. 24, translation HB). He laments the extreme specialisation in the study of nature in contemporary culture, even chastising it as a unique duplicity, for while it offers many merits, it is also characterised by incoherence. He points out that those who work on the frontiers of one field of research ignore and often mock work taking place at other frontiers. Further, he writes: "With regard to time, the extravagance is that both disciplines deal with the same natural event; some in order to deny it as an illusion, others in order to study it more and more thoroughly, reducing it to nervous physic-chemical events" (p. 24, translation HB).

Without denying the findings of modern physics, he refers to the evolution of the nervous system and the brain: "Time became part of the phenomenology of life when, in the course of evolution, nervous mechanisms began to transmit it to the brain areas of animal consciousness and human self-consciousness, a process that developed over tens of thousands of centuries" (2020, p. 56). With a similar view of Hawking, he continues, "The reflection based on the Big Bang, on what was there before the origin of time, is sterile: the time on which self-conscious mankind reflects has existed since the brain started to make it a reality of consciousness, and therefore a dimension of life and the universe." He goes on to say:

Wondering what time was like immediately after or shortly after the Big Bang, and what time is like in other galaxies does not lead anywhere, since the only time of which we can be aware is that of the present and here on Earth. When we say that the Big Bang, the birth of the universe, took place 13.5 billion years ago, we are projecting backwards, from the only dimension of which we are aware, to the present time. And in the case of inhabited planets in distant galaxies, the time is the time processed by the brains – if they have any – of their inhabitants. And if we ever reach them, we will retain our sense of time there too. Genes transmit the nervous system mechanisms of the sense of time from one generation to the next. In humans it becomes manifest in about the third year of life, together with memory, which is one of the bases of time.

(2020, pp. 56/57, translation HB)

He acknowledges the differences between "*governmental time*" (the official time standard used by a government for official and legal purposes), *personal time* and *timing*. A central conclusion of Benini's is this:

> Within the sense of space is placed what is perceived, while time is always only felt – it doesn't come from experience and but mechanisms of the brain. The centres of space are congenital and, in humans, need time to mature with experience. This is unlike in mice, where they mature a couple of days after birth. The centres of space present an interesting analogy with the centres of language that arise with a particular nervous structure, which, for Noam Chomsky, is the anatomical basis of the universal grammar, and present only in human beings. It comes into operation only if and when stimulated by the language of the environment in which it grows. There is no spontaneous language of the brain. There is the highly specific and uniquely human nervous structure to acquire one, and even more than one. *The sense of time is present even without experience of space.*

(2020, p. 125, italics and translation HB)

Let us now turn to history, which has great significance for psychoanalysts, just as the biological and psychological foundations of life do. As a historian, François Hartog has addressed the significance of time, especially in occidental culture, and I will offer a few introductory remarks here.

Hartog starts from what he calls "the ineductible present" and sees our contemporary period as shaped by a "presentism" which valorises the present (2020, p. 276). He gives as example Vladimir and Estragon in Beckett's 1952 play, *En Attendant Godot*; for these two "heroes", time does not pass – "*le temps s'est arrêté*" – "time has stopped". For them, the days pass and do not pass. Is it the night that arrives or the day that begins? They are completely disoriented in time and space.

With the Western world after Auschwitz and Hiroshima, he sees a "new presentism" which time has similarly stopped, "like a picture that has been frozen". While on one hand, this halt of time could be described as an ethical order (2020, p. 274), however, in the following years, the present became "fashionable and very quickly an imperative: one must not only be of one's time but work and live in the present. The word 'present' is valorised. Never be at rest, be flexible, mobile, responding to demand, innovating without pause – these are its watchwords" (2020, p. 276).

Against this backdrop, Hartog goes in search of "lost time" – "*les temps perdu*" – and turns to "long journeys in time" (2020, p. 9/10) only to return to the present. He examines "Chronos", ancient time; and describes how the Occident has struggled with time in the course of different "regimes of historicity", from the Greek through the Christian epochs to the present day. The concept of "*régime d'historicité*" – "regime of historicity[4]" – allows us to investigate crucial moments of social change in different epochs and to discover how these moments relate to the past, present and future.

The successor of the Greek epoch was the Christian regime of historicity from which the modern era and our contemporary society have evolved. Hartog sees Chronos as omnipresent and inescapable, but one which can't be grasped, but also one which human have never given up on mastering. Distinguishing between "the order of time" and "epochs of time", Hartog proposes going from the Greek way of understanding Chronos, with its splitting of time into an immutable divine eternity and a perishable human existence, to the serious contemporary uncertainties, with a long halt at the time of the Christians, conceived of and established by the nascent church, a present caught between the Incarnation and the Last Judgement. This, he describes as the "march" of Western time and also the Occident's struggle with time.

To map the ruptures and transitions between the epochs – from antiquity to Christianity, the Renaissance, the modern era and our time – Hartog uses conceptual terms in a particular way. He puts Chronos between "Kairos", the auspicious moment, and "Krisis", crisis. He further differentiates a Christian form of "presentism" from our contemporary, demanding version and speaks of our new time as "Anthropocene". He describes "how the hold of Christian time spread and imposed itself, before it declined in the face of modern time, driven by progress and moving rapidly towards the future." However, this future, he continues, "has darkened and a new time has arisen, quickly designated as the 'Anthropocene', the name of a new geological era in which the human species has become the main force, a geological force." He asks: "What then becomes of the old ways of grasping Chronos, what new strategies should be formulated to face this immeasurable and threatening future, even though we are more or less hemmed in by the evanescent and constraining time of what I have called presentism?" (2020, from the back cover, translation HB).

After describing the Christian mechanisms of *accomodatio*, where God adapts to man; *reformatio*, where this accommodation is reformed; *translatio*, which transforms the political order; and *renovatio*, the birth of man in Christ – or, if in antiquity, in Christianity – Hartog moves towards a restitution of Chronos for our present time. Now that the climate threat has succeeded the nuclear threat and the economy is hard to control, we are living in a state of permanent crisis. Instead of Kairos, we are dealing with Krisis in capitalism and teetering on the verge of a new apocalypse. Hartog agrees with Latour, who pleads for a new presentism that is not Christian but infused with its ethical and spiritual qualities. Otherwise, as Günther Anders said, are not the "apocalypticists" basically "prophylacticists" who prevent the apocalypse? This would offer the moment where Kairos returns amidst Krisis. He wonders if the COVID-19 pandemic could also be a Kairos amidst Krisis.

To know Kairos is one thing: to translate it into action is another and raises questions such as: Which actions? And with or without violence? He returns to another Greek concept which inscribes itself between Kairos and Krisis – stasis: "How to influence the crisis, how to go towards the crisis? By translating, by setting up the kairos-occasion as a stasis, whether we understand it as a confrontation, a class struggle, a civil war . . . This path is known, and its risks too" (2020 p. 335, translation HB).

In contrast to the extensive overview of the background to the three keynote papers so far, I will no more than touch briefly on the thoughts of psychoanalyst Bernd Nissen (2014), allowing for the fullness of his detailed conceptual reflections later in this book. Nissen names rhythm and flow as the two qualities that Freud associates with the psyche/mind. His thesis is that for Freud, the timelessness of the unconscious cannot be grasped as the absence of any phenomena similar to time. He places great emphasis on mental states in which the dichotomy between conscious and unconscious, between subject and object and the opposition of self and world is suspended. In such states, everything appears with greater clarity and contour, and he suggests these states could be described as "presence". According to Bion, such experiences and transformations in O cannot be produced, even less can they be forced. As human beings, we can only be seized by presence. Nissen too uses the term "Kairos" for these moments. Evocatively, he says pure presence is paradoxical at the moment of its experience: it is without name, at the same time enabling precise meaning; it is without evaluation; and everything is simultaneously there and not there.

In summary, Freud conceives of time as the conscious flow from which past, present and future emerge, while the timelessness of the unconscious is rhythmic, circular, periodic and repetitive. During experiences of presence in O, being and time meet – being happens and time is there. These experiences of time are thought to be circular and paradoxical, and Nissen illustrates this with clinical examples, especially drawn from psychotic and autistoid states.

In one of his other publications, Nissen also cites the presence of death as summoning such experiences. Connections between the theme of time and the topic of death have been made by several authors, also in this volume. Hawking and Mlodinow include the ideas of reaching an end and death within the concept of an arrow of time. Rovelli, too, concluded his book with his subjective fearlessness before death. For us psychoanalysts, the realm of time is, on one hand, profoundly linked to the processes of and possibilities for psychic change; but also, to the recognition of termination of treatment, loss and mourning and death.

To conclude this introductory chapter, I'd like to share a vignette from the analysis of a child which lasted from the seventh to the tenth year of his life. This boy, who I will call Eric, had an implicit idea of change over time. From a current moment, he could look back to our earlier sessions; he could also develop phantasmic conceptions of himself and me in future encounters. In psychoanalysis, we are working with the present, the past and the potential future of our patients. In analytic processes with adults, we often deal with the presence of the infantile past even if we do not forget the future. But in the treatment of children and adolescents, we are often more directly confronted with the presence of their potential future, even as we do not forget their prior experiences (cp. Blass, 2021). In the analysis with Eric, this switching between the present, past and future was a central part of his development.

While I'm unable to reveal much about his or his parents' reasons for contacting me, I can perhaps only mention that he was often unable to control his feelings and manage his affective expressions; he had serious difficulties at school and in his interactions with other children. Gradually, over time, he developed a trusting relationship with me and found space for himself and access to his feelings within the density of four hours per week. The longer he came and the better he got too, the more often he asked me how many sessions had passed between us and how much time still lay ahead. It was important to him to record what had already happened and what would happen between us in the future because he repeatedly stated that he wanted to come until he was at least eighteen.

The extent to which the dimension of time played a role in his development is exemplified by a letter he wrote to me in the second year of his analysis before the long summer holidays began. Here is my translation of the letter:

> For Heribert. Dear Heribert, I am sorry I have to leave you – I am going on a big trip around the world. But in ten years I'll be back. I am going to China, Japan, USA, Germany, the East – just look around the whole world – once around the globe and I'll be glad when we meet again – when I come back I'm 52 years old and you are 29 years old – many greetings, your father.

Additionally, he drew two footballers important to him and wrote their age as nineteen, which was much younger than the reality.

The letter demonstrates how he dealt with the disappointment and pain of the separation: namely, by turning passivity into activity and making himself the one who left me, who further grew older and even became my father. He reversed the generational order, and playing with time in this way helped him a great deal. It felt, as if Eric was able to make use of the relativity of time, and unconsciously he already seemed to know that there is no such thing as absolute time.

Another episode also illustrates how he handled time in his mind to help regulate his affects. Once, when I pointed out the sad but inevitable end of the session, which he didn't want to accept, he finally put on his jacket and said on his way out, "Bye! See you at your funeral. I will dance on your grave." He combined his anger and disappointment with a triumph over me in the future. I could only confirm this eventual future for him but told him he would have to wait a little until that time arrived. The next day, he was worried and said it had all been fun.

Like in the work with young Eric, the importance of the concept of time in psychoanalysis cannot be overstated. As analysts, we sense and conceptualise the here and now of the relationship with our analysands in the session, but we always include past and possible future moments, both in our mutual contact and in their lifetime to come beyond the consulting room. Our experience of time in psychoanalysis is also significantly influenced by the nature of the relationship between analysand and analyst.

The contributions that follow will examine more fully the sometimes incomprehensible phenomenon of time from a range of perspectives. As with the editors' reflections at the end of this book, we hope these writings will stimulate and inspire further thoughts in the reader's mind.

Notes

1 "Murder of time" refers to the way certain psychic mechanisms distort or annihilate the experience of time. It is often linked to conditions such as depression, severe trauma or psychosis, where the ordinary flow of time – past, present and future – becomes disrupted. It can also be seen as an expression of internal destructive processes – some also speak of the death drive – which undermine(s) life's forward momentum and vitality. Instead of progression, there is a regressive pull towards stasis or obliteration. It can result in feelings of timelessness or eternity that are not liberating but suffocating and deadening.

2 While the "murder of time" refers to the annihilation or stagnation of temporal experience, "exploded time" focuses on the chaotic disintegration of the normal flow of time in the psyche. Instead of experiencing time as a cohesive, linear progression, individuals may feel as though they are stuck in fragmented, disconnected moments.

3 In psychoanalysis, "reaction formation" is a defence mechanism identified by Sigmund Freud wherein a person unconsciously replaces an unacceptable thought, feeling or impulse with its opposite. This serves to avoid the anxiety or guilt associated with the original desire. Examples would be a person who harbours a pronounced hostility towards another person and then becomes particularly friendly.

4 Historicity is the quality of being a real and important part of history and not a myth or legend. The Blackwell Dictionary of Western Philosophy defines historicity as "denoting the feature of our human situation by which we are located in specific concrete temporal and historical circumstances."

References

Benini, A. (2020). *Neurobiologia del tempo.* Milano: Raffaello Cortina Editore

Blass, H. (2021). The adult future of the child, the infantile past of the adult and the psychoanalytic process (Unpublished lecture International Psychoanalytical Congress 2021, online)

Canestri, J. & Glocer Fiorini, L. (2018 [2009]). Introduction: The experience of time. In: Glocer Fiorini, L. & Canestri, J. (eds), *The Experience of Time. Psychoanalytic Perspectives.* London and New York: Routledge, xxiii–xxix

Green, A. (2003). Zeitlichkeit in der Psychoanalyse: zersplitterte Zeit. *Psyche – Z Psychoanal* 57, 789–811

Green, A. (2018 [2009]). From the ignorance of time to the murder of time. From the murder of time to the misrecognition of temporality in psychoanalysis. In: Glocer Fiorini, L. & Canestri, J. (eds), *The Experience of Time. Psychoanalytic Perspectives.* London and New York: Routledge, 1–19

Hanly, C. (2018 [2009]). A problem with Freud's idea oft he timelessness of the unconscious. In: Glocer Fiorini, L. & Canestri, J. (eds), *The Experience of Time. Psychoanalytic Perspectives.* London and New York: Routledge, 21–34

Hartog, F. (2020). *Chronos. L'Occident aux prises avec le Temps.* Éditions Gallimard

Hawking, S. & Mlodinow, L. (2005). *The Shortest History of Time.* Reinbek by Hamburg: Rowohlt

Loewald, H. (1972). The experience of time (1972). *Psychoanal. Study Child* 27, 401–410

Münster. G. (2010). *Was ist die Zeit? nachgefragt, Dialogverlag 2010.* https://www.uni-muenster.de/Physik.TP/~munsteg/10Zeit.pdf

Nissen, B. (2014). Versuch einer psychoanalytischen Theorie der Zeit. Zeitschrift für psychoanalytische Theorie und Praxis. *Jahrgang* XXIX, 279–298

Rovelli, C. (2019). *The order of time.* UK: Penguin Books

Chapter 2

Science, psychoanalysis and the time of the session

Leopoldo Bleger

Debate continues to rage about whether psychoanalysis is a science or not. It seems certain to me that a certain scientific spirit has largely ordered its development right from the days of Sigmund Freud. Consider his concern for observation and its difficulties, and a clear distinction between this endeavour and speculation ("Beyond the Pleasure Principle"); his recognition of the problem of description (his remark on Rome in "Civilisation and its Discontents"); his questioning of the foundations of theory ("Instincts and their Vicissitudes"); and similarly, the careful thought given by him and later thinkers to the creation of hypotheses, and the seriousness of what is articulated and the logic crafting it. Whether psychoanalysis itself is science or not, Freud's approach is therefore scientific.

More lately, we are also confronted with the epistemological obstacle raised by Gaston Bachelard regarding the curious relationship between the investigator and his object – i.e. one observes an object with the object itself. The object in our work is the unconscious; it commands and drives our investigations while simultaneously imposing its conditions and limiting what can be known about it. The psychoanalytic methods of free association and attention in equal suspension allow a certain form of access to the unconscious.

Science itself and the various sciences continue to inspire psychoanalysis. Thinking of psychoanalysis as one among the sciences, Freud borrowed notions such as force, work, energy and others from the physics of his time. How often he paused his pen and asked other sciences for new hypotheses on which to base developments in his own thinking! Freud's initial training, and indeed his vocation, was that of a scientist. His early work was as a bench researcher, and he was inspired by the discoveries of his time. A clear example is the extraordinary text that is the "Project"

DOI: 10.4324/9781003660118-2

("*Entwurf*"); it is the consequence, among other things, of the description of the neuron by Ramón y Cajal in 1880. As with DNA, these findings facilitated major advances.

In the tradition of modern science, Freud begins his major works with a bibliographical review – where do we start from, what has been said about it, the difficulties and so on. His book on dreams begins with an extensive survey of the literature about it. "Totem and Taboo" is based on the anthropology and evolutionary theory of its time; the same goes for "Group Psychology" and the second part of "Beyond the Pleasure Principle". For the reader of today, many of the references he drew upon might seem dusty or even downright wacky, but some are still surprisingly relevant. For example, Weismann's germ cell theory, which proposes a certain form of immortality of the cell, seems to still be on the agenda for contemporary scientists.[1]

Freud sought out new ideas from other sciences; he was inspired by the emerging hypotheses and used them, even twisting concepts if needed. But there was never a question of following others or yielding to the diktats of another discipline; he had his own field of elaboration – his clinic, which Pontalis called "the central laboratory."[2] There was also no question of trying to subsume psychoanalysis into another science or a broader whole – rather, his idea was to make psychoanalysis the basis of another science, and he embarked on numerous projects towards this end. The best-known attempt is "Ego Psychology", whose scope was intended to include and unify medicine, psychiatry and psychology on a new basis.[3]

Almost at every step, Freud questions what he is doing or about to do. This is certainly a scientific approach, but it also shows the acute difficulty of transmitting such a singular science, one which is bound to provoke resistance. As has been already noticed, Freud seems to write in dialogue or debate with an interlocutor, an objector even.

Other disciplines have continued to inspire psychoanalysis, and this has been particularly apparent in France, where "structural linguistics" and anthropology had a profound impact on the elaborations of the 1950s and 1960s, notably in Lacan's work. Faced with criticism, Lacan replied that he was not doing linguistics but "linguisterie", implying that he was appropriating linguistics for his own creative ends. At the same time, it is evident that researchers in the hard sciences often don't proceed according to the idealised image that many laymen, including psychoanalysts, have of them: methodological rigour with adherence to evidence and experimentation that walks the tightrope of both testing and challenging the boundaries of what is known.

While we have been recalling the historical relationship between psychoanalysis and the sciences, in recent years, two trends have become marked in the analytic world. The first is a jealous retreat into the specificity and singularity of the analytic approach, a fierce defence against anything that aims at collapsing the space psychoanalysis has created. On the other hand, there is a major tendency to use the data of new sciences towards re-founding psychoanalysis on other bases, nowadays neuroscience.

Freud himself did not escape this tension (*tiraillement* in French) between the non-reducible specificity of psychoanalysis and the advances of science from its physical and chemical foundations. His participation in the Helmholtz school with du Bois-Reymond, Carl Ludwig and others is well known; this was a programme to reduce all human phenomena to physic-chemical bases. Although recalling this might trouble or disturb many psychoanalysts, I think it is fortunate that Freud had had the training of a scientist. What might have happened to the experience acquired little by little in his clinic without this scientific spirit?

Erwin Schrödinger's famous 1944 lecture, "What is Life?",[4,5] unreservedly revived this programme, and it remains relevant today. So much the better, for I do not see how any aspect of scientific life could proceed otherwise. The difficulties begin when the scientific position becomes an ideology. Freud did not wish to turn psychoanalysis into a worldview; rather, he wanted the conception of psychoanalysis to only be in the field of science, made up of attempts, hypotheses and profound revisions. It is impossible for us to know what will be the fate of this programme that promises the certain death of psychoanalysis. While the death of psychoanalysis has been foretold so often that it has acquired the air of the ridiculous, we are aware that the *practice* of psychoanalysis can be destroyed.

Here is one such moment when the edifice falters. In "On Narcissism: an Introduction", the epistemological and methodological question is continually present, announcing in a way the opening of metapsychology in the reflections of "Instincts and their Vicissitudes". It might be wondered why we do not rally to Jung's position of a unitary psychic energy – is this an abandonment of observation for barren theoretical controversy? While a speculative theory would propose a sharply defined concept as its basis, here is a science built on "empirical interpretation" ("interpretation" and not mere fact) – nebulous, barely imaginable basic concepts, which one hopes to apprehend more clearly in due course. Freud held that "it is observation alone" which is the foundation of science, not these ideas. He added that the physics of his time was experiencing the same radical change in fundamental concepts like matter, centres of force, attraction etc. This astonishing remark from 1914 shows that he was well aware of what was happening in science.

Since we do not have a theory of the instincts, Freud continues, we make the attempt with a hypothesis and pursue it until it either breaks down or is confirmed. He reiterates that our conceptions in psychology are provisional and

> will presumably someday be based on an organic substructure. This makes it probable that it is special substances and chemical processes which perform the operations of sexuality and provide for the extension of individual life into that of the species. We are taking this probability into account in replacing the special chemical substances by special psychical forces.[6,7]

Freud kept this question of instincts open until the end of his work but changed his mind about the place of speculation six years later (1920, Chapter 3 of "Beyond the Pleasure Principle").

It would be too much to hope that the questions psychoanalysis posits about time and its different modalities might speak to other disciplines. This has been the case previously but perhaps is no longer so; only time will tell.

To remember that psychoanalysis is a science and to keep in mind its beginnings allows us to understand that we are necessarily situated somewhere in this history. Contrary to what we prefer to believe, our thinking operates with a certain number of elements; our readings are necessarily oriented; and our assumptions are a mixture of perception and thought but also prejudice and haste.

*

From the broad brushstrokes of history and the sweeping development of conceptual thinking, I'd like to reflect on the microcosm of psychoanalytic treatment itself as it happens. In their account of the psychoanalytic cure and the elaboration they propose, some analysts are able to make us feel the space of the session, the time of the cure and everything that happens in a subterranean way. We are also aware that the psychoanalytic cure takes place beyond the avatars of each session, of this or that dream, of an interpretation (and we never know how far an interpretation carries, if it does at all); what is central is the continuity of the sessions, the regularity of the encounters, a repetition, an analyst who is there but also not available the rest of the time – very present during the session but whose separations and absences punctuate the time of a treatment. It is difficult to show the great movements of the treatment, the more or less immobile part which cannot really be captured in the moment. Sometimes, the stakes of a treatment are not at all where we think they are.

It is the length of time allowed for the bringing into play (*mise en jeu*) of instinctual forces (*Triebregungen*) in the transferential movements. The temporality of the analytic situation is strange, made up of moments when an interpretation, sometimes a single word, prompts a rather marked turn against a background of a stretch of time. Or rather, it should be said that it is precisely because we give ourselves all the time we need that these lightning moments can appear. It is probably an error in perspective that gives too much importance to what we can grasp and name while we remain ignorant of large parts of a treatment.

It is the changes, the more or less abrupt variations in the same session, that should hold our attention – this we all know from our practice and also our own analysis. This "shattered time", to use André Green's term, is one of the characteristics of time in psychoanalysis – and yet it's not necessarily shattered. Sometimes, there's an acceleration in the last few minutes of the session because we think we have grasped something – that this patient acts as if separations do not exist, so she doesn't need to hold on to the relationship or the contact.

Theory and metapsychology – that theory with a special status that Freud invented – only partially accounts for this experience, whose profound quality we consider to be "Erlebnis". Both patients and analysts experience strange phenomena; they are what allow the analytical treatment to take place. Sometimes, it is the experience of time being suspended, where the time of the session no longer seems to exist; at times, there is the particular pain of the repetition compulsion – a configuration that repeats itself tirelessly.

The end of an analytical treatment throws the matter of time into sharp relief. I am reminded of a patient who was very affected when the question of the end of her analysis came up – the thought of actually finishing this analysis terrified her, but perhaps even more, the sense that it would not be endless. It marked a turning point in her process with its massive inhibitions, and she was finally able to think of a direction for her work. She said being able to imagine that one day, the analysis would end felt to her like the world would end. She then associated to the early days of her analysis: for a very long time (and perhaps still), she was really convinced that a small painting in my office was also in her childhood home. She said analysis was a space-time! That formula strikes me as accurate, indicating the strangeness of the analytical session.

The practice of psychoanalysis is founded on the time of each singular human origin, the precocious flowering of infantile sexual life. We might think of it as a little or even completely out of time – it is a flowering doomed to failure as the child does not have the means to fulfil his desires. This is the basis of both the unhappiness of the adult and the possibility of his psychic elaboration. We could say "felix" precocity and this time lag marks every human being until death. We live the present with those first glasses of childhood, and our future is infused with a tireless return to those earliest days.

*

To conclude, I would like to return to Jose Canestri, who conceived of this interdisciplinary symposium and chose the theme of time. The range of literature that has been contributed, particularly from biology and physics, affirms the interest in what he proposed. It also demonstrates that there can be no possibility of aiming for a unified vision of the question of time. By its sheer magnitude and its difficulties, the theme inherently discourages any unifying attempt. A logical positivist is likely to tell me that this shows that the problem is badly posed – he would probably not be wrong.

On the division I mentioned earlier between the fierce defenders of the absolute specificity of psychoanalysis and those who are on the side of opening up to new sciences, Jorge Canestri's position was clear and firm. He was just as jealous of the analytical thing and its practice, as he was a man of knowledge, curious about the latest news in science – science in the making. He was something of a Renaissance man from before the partition of the sciences. It is when the positions, both sides, are held firmly together that the exchange can take place.

Notes

1 Le Douarin, N. (2019). *Les secrets de la vie*. CNRS Edition
2 Pontalis, J.-B. (2012). *Le laboratoire central*. Ed. de l'Olivier
3 Loewenstein, R., Newman, L., Schur, M. & Solnit, A. (eds). (1966). *Psychoanalysis- A General Psychology. Essays in Honor of Heinz Hartmann*. New York: International University Press
4 Bernfeld, S. (1944). Freud earliest theories and the school of Helmholtz. *The Psychoanal. Quart.* 13(3), 341–362
5 Erwin Schrödinger's book was published in 1944, a few years before DNA and the way it reproduces itself could be described. He questions at the outset: "How can physics and chemistry account for the space-time events that take place within the boundaries of a living organism?" In other words, he questions the programme that Freud too experienced during the years of his scientific training. This is the Schrödinger who went on to become one of the principal contributors to the development of quantum mechanics and also gave us the famous conundrum of the cat that is dead and alive at the same time. In his introduction, he adds that the inability of the chemistry and physics of the time to account for his facts is no reason to doubt that these sciences will be able to account for them at some point in the future.
6 Pour introduire le narcissisme. *OCP* XII, 220–222, *GW* X, 141–144, *SE* XIV, 77
7 Pour introduire le narcissisme. *OCP* XII, 220–222, *GW* X, 141–144, *SE* XIV, 77, 78 (*SE*). I'm quoting Strachey's translation, which does not seem very accurate!

References

Bernfeld, S. (1944). Freud earliest theories and the school of Helmholtz. *The Psychoanal. Quart.* 13(3), 341–362
Freud, S. (1914). On narcissism. An introduction. *SE* XIV, 67–102
Freud, S. (1920). *Au-delà du principe de plaisir*. OCP XV, 273–338, GW XIII, 3–69, SE XVIII, 7–64.
Le Douarin, N. (2019). *Les secrets de la vie*. CNRS Edition
Loewenstein, R., Newman, L., Schur, M. & Solnit, A. (eds). (1966). *Psychoanalysis- A General Psychology. Essays in Honor of Heinz Hartmann*. New York: International University Press
Pontalis, J.-B. (2012). *Le laboratoire central*. Ed. de l'Olivier

Chapter 3

Neurobiology of time

Arnaldo Benini

An apparently banal experience: when we look at the clock, our consciousness assigns a numerical value, but to what? When we look at it
later, we measure an interval, a duration. What has been measured? Time.
Time can be imagined as a one-dimensional line of an infinite sequence
of its constituent elements: the *instants*. The topological structure of time
is *dense*, compact, since between two instants, there are infinite others,
even if the amount of time between two instants is not infinite. The length
of an interval is not determined by the number of instants (Arntzenius,
2012). It would be absurd to maintain, according to the mathematician
and philosopher Bernard Bolzano, "that in a short duration the same set of
instants is contained as in a longer duration, or that the infinite intervals
of time in which a short duration can be decomposed to have the same
length as those in which a longer duration can be divided into" (Bolzano,
1965, p. 102). Nothing that is perceived of the world has a similar nature,
confirming that time is not in the world, even if this does not mean that it
is a *nonentity*.

Time is elusive: we don't see it, we don't touch it, we don't smell it,
we don't hear it like we hear a sound. But it is real. Our conscience *feels
it* (does not *perceive it*) as part of itself. The elusive nature of time has
made it difficult to define its nature, origin and meaning: time, writes the
philosopher Vladimir Jankélévitch, "is never an object exhibited before
us, present in place in space, as are the mines of mineralogy [. . .] you
can't reproduce its shape, because it has no shape" (Jankélévitch, 1987,
p. 166). Nevertheless, as neurobiological research (which not only the
philosophers but also the physicians, *more solito*, ignore) has studied and

DOI: 10.4324/9781003660118-3

found in the central nervous system of humans and animals: the sense of time is real.

It is an event of consciousness. Temporality is a fundamental determinant of existence: experience is temporally structured, and temporality is the trellis of every cognitive event (Shanon, 2001). Moreover, comparative neurobiology demonstrates and confirms that there are no beings with a central nervous system that have no sense of time: without it, their life is not imaginable.

What is time? A short history

What is time and where does it come from?

Many philosophers, from Plato to Paul Ricoeur, have written wonderful texts on time which, however, say nothing about its nature and origins. The only exception is Immanuel Kant. Neuroscience proves fully Kant's opinion that time is not an attribute of the universe that we perceive; it rather is in our inner sense: therefore, time is felt, not perceived.

Up to David Hume, reflections on time, like those of Newton and Leibniz, had mainly religious connotations, which were based on Plato's conception according to which "the days and the nights, the months and the years" had been created by the Demiurge, by the Maker, that is, by God, when he created the world. And with the world they would end (Plato, ca. 360 B.C.E.).

According to Hume, time is an empirical concept due to the perceptible succession of changing objects. We perceive it, for Hume (1975), as a component of the world of which we have experience, so it is impossible to conceive of a time without succession or change to something that really exists. Claiming that time is produced by the relationships between the objects of perception and in reference to those who perceive them, Hume did not consider that there is a sense of time even if nothing moves and changes and when nothing is perceived. A person "immersed in a deep sleep," he writes, "is insensitive to time": he could not have known that the sense of time works and conditions us even during sleep (Hume, 1975, p. 48).

Immanuel Kant laid the conceptual foundation on which the neurobiological research of the sense of time would then develop. Unlike Hume, time, for Kant, is not an empirical concept derived from experience. On the contrary, mental events as well as the experience of the world, which is acquired with the sense organs and elaborated with the mechanisms of perception, are inserted into the cognitive pillars of existence, one of which is the sense of time, whose foundation is memory. For Kant (1787), time is a "form of our inner sense, [. . .] a pure form of sensitive intuition, and not something that exists for itself in the world. It is a condition a priori of all appearances in general." And, he adds: "The order and regularity of appearances, which we call nature, are [. . .] ourselves to introduce them. On the other hand, we certainly could not find them in nature, if we ourselves [. . .] had not originally introduced them" (Kant, 1787/1977, p. 80). Time, therefore, is not an attribute of the universe that we perceive but is in us, in our *inneren Sinn*. Therefore, time is felt, not perceived.

G.W.F. Hegel wrote one of the best syntheses of Kant's original idea about time and space.

> Time and space are the a priori forms of perception . . . all that we perceive is transferred in congenital, a priori categories of time and space. Therefore, time and space are not empiric . . . Consciousness has in itself space and time. We cannot imagine things out of time and space. Time and space make experience possible like mouth and teeth make eating possible.
>
> (Hegel, 1975, p. 103)

Temps perdu traced by H. von Helmholtz and B. Libet

The sense of time is in us, in our body. But where? This was the first question of neuroscience about time. The basics of the neurobiology of time was intuited and experimented by Hermann von Helmholtz 1849 and fully confirmed 130 years later by Benjamin Libet.

The sense of time is innate in us, in our body. But where is it? Kant's intuition of the *internal sense* of time was confirmed by a German scientist who was, not surprisingly, Kant's scholar (Benini, 2020b; Cahan, 2018; Finkelstein, 2013; Norton Wise, 2018). In 1849, Hermann von Helmholtz, in an extraordinary creative outburst, intuited, experimented and described the basics of the neurobiology of time, confirmed to this day. Using a device perfected by Emil du Bois-Reymond, he stimulated the nerve of a frog's gastrocnemius muscle prepared for dissection and recorded the muscle response.

At the time, it was an undisputed belief that the electrical stimulation of a motor nerve and the contraction of the muscle were simultaneous. This was by virtue of the "imponderable principle", belonging only to animals and plants, of the *Lebenskraft*, vitality, exclusive life energy. This vitalistic concept, however, has never been proven.

The gastrocnemius muscle of a frog's paw is stretched between a fixed bar, at the top, and a moving bar, at the bottom. The tip of the latter marks the path in a smoked cylinder. The electrical stimulus is given simultaneously to the iliac plexus or the sciatic nerve of the leg and the cylinder, which starts to rotate. The bar does not rise immediately, simultaneously to the stimulus, as should have happened if the electrified stimulus and muscle contraction had been simultaneous, but after a little interval, the longer the stimulated nerve, i.e. the muscle did not begin to contract immediately upon being stimulated. Helmholtz drew his new finding: "[. . .]the Energie (the strength) of the muscle does not completely develop in the moment of an instant excitation but largely only after the excitation is already ceased does it gradually increase, reach a maximum and then disappear again" (Helmholtz, 1850, p. 363).

The moment the muscle begins to contract to reach maximum strength, electric stimulation of the nerve is interrupted, while the current that spins the cylinder continues. The muscle contracts, the bar rises, stays at that level for the time of contraction, and then the muscle becomes relaxed, and the lever drops. The horizontal stretch between the start of electrical stimulation and the beginning of the contraction is the latency between stimulus and muscle contraction, which our sense organs do not perceive: it is the time needed for the stimulus to run along the nerve and get to the muscle. "I found," von Helmholtz writes in a first, succinct account of the experiment, "that a measurable time passes during which an electrical stimulus reaches the nerve of the frog's muscle" (Helmholtz, 1850c/1895, pp. 3, 71). In a nerve 50 to 60 mm long, stimulated at a temperature between 11 and 15 degrees Celsius, he measured an interval that goes from 0.0014 to 0.0020 seconds.

Twenty years before Marcel Proust's birth, Hermann von Helmholtz called the latency between stimulus and muscle contraction *temps perdu*, time that exists but which is lost to consciousness (and therefore to memory) because it is not perceived. Today, the technical term for such latency is *"compressed time"* because it is a time that exists and is measured, even if compressed by the brain's mechanisms to such an extent that it is imperceptible.

Subjective simultaneity is an illusion, a cerebral interpretation that manipulates events and physical signals of the world.

In his wider work on the subject, von Helmholtz reiterates how his experiences confirm the Kantian vision of time, space and causality (Helmholtz, 1921, p. 109). Those are not in the world but are the product of the brain and of the central nervous system of all living beings with a nervous system.

Hermann von Helmholtz corroborated the mechanical vision of nature's events and, therefore, the reduction of consciousness to the physical-chemical mechanisms of the brain. With him and his Berliner colleague and friend, du Bois-Reymond, physiology and biology already were placed definitively on a scientific basis and subtracted from religious views and speculative theories.

The *"reaction time"* of Benjamin Libet. The illusion of the present

We are aware of the sensory and mental experience not when it happens but about half a second later. We have no awareness of the long latency. If we had it, it would probably be unpleasant. In evolution, a mechanism has prevailed that scrapes the retroactive referral time. This is the time it takes the associative cortex to make stimuli and mental events conscious. This time is then compressed. The present is always past.

Hermann von Helmholtz had shown that the mechanisms of the sense of time are in the brain. The brain can distort time, because it is itself that creates it and then communicates it to the mechanisms of consciousness. The brain makes us live in an illusory simultaneity between events and the consciousness we have. The experience is summarized in Figure 3.1, one of the most famous curves of neuroscience (Libet et al., 1979).

In 1979, Benjamin Libet confirmed the *"reaction time,"* which corresponds to von Helmholtz's *temps perdu*, that is, the illusion of the simultaneity between stimulus and consciousness of it, with his experiences using the equipment of his time, later confirmed by the most sophisticated *neuroimaging*.

The tactile feeling is taken as an example, but the data applies to all kinds of sensitivities: if you are touched on your hand (or if you touch

Retroactive referral (antedating) of subjective sensory experience

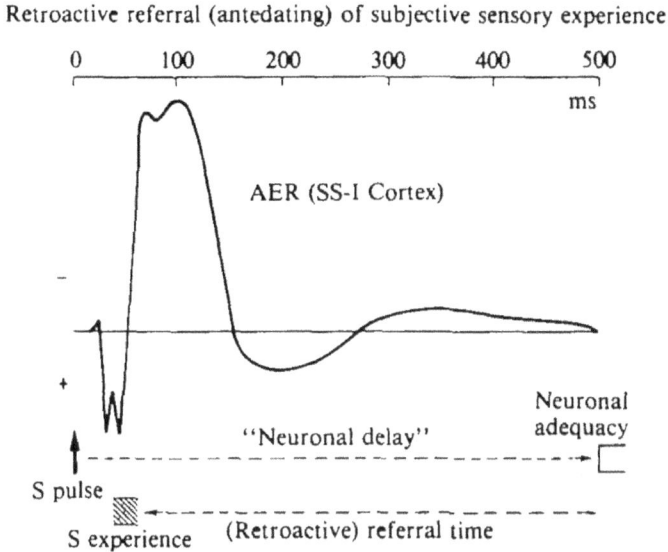

Figure 3.1 See text. The recording of cortical electrical activity takes place, in waking time, through a drill hole practiced for stereotaxic operation. (Figure 2 from Libet et al. (1979, p. 201). Reproduced with permission.)

something) or on a foot or any other part of the body, you are sure to be aware of it in the act in which this takes place. In fact, the sequence goes differently: touching (upwards arrow to the left) stimulates the tactile nerves, and their stimulus reaches the contralateral somato-sensory cortex after 14 to 20 milliseconds if the stimulus comes from the hand or after 40 to 50 milliseconds if it comes from the foot due to the different distance that the impulse must travel in the nerves and spinal cord. The potentials thus evoked in the cortex, whose amplitude depends on the strength of peripheral stimulation, are different from the cortical activity produced by directly stimulating the cortex with electric discharges.

After about a tenth of a second, the primary somatosensory area has finished its work, and the stimulus continues towards the associative areas of consciousness, which take part in the cerebral cortex and subcortical structures. It is active after about half a second. It is a long latency, of which we are not aware. Being touched and the awareness of the event are seemingly simultaneous, even if we are touched in areas very differently far from the brain such as the face, hand and foot. The brain does not transmit to the mechanisms of consciousness the half a second to process the stimulus coming from the periphery until it becomes conscious nor the difference between the length of the path of the stimulation of the hand and that of the foot. How the compression of time affects existence is unclear, although many (or perhaps all) of the brain areas in which it takes place have been identified. If, at the same time as the tapping of the hand (or foot or any other part of the body), it electrically stimulates its area in the cortical somatosensory exposed for the stereotaxic operation, the touching of the hand is felt *before* the tear or stitch by cortical electrical stimulation, because, unlike the time of direct stimulation of the cortex, the time of stimulation from the hand to the brain is compressed. The cerebral mechanisms of time compression act on stimuli from the periphery to the brain and not on those from the somaticcortical area to the periphery. The neuronal delay between the event of sensory stimulation and the consciousness of it is called by Libet retroactive referral time: that is, retroactive reference, of which there is no awareness and, therefore, it does not enter into the memory. The compression of that space of time indicates that there is always half a second of delay before we become aware.

We are aware of the sensory experience not when it happens but about half a second later. We have no awareness of the long latency, which would probably be quite unpleasant. For this reason, in evolution, a mechanism has prevailed that shortens the retroactive referral time, the time it takes the associative cortex to make stimuli conscious. The unconscious compression of that time means that we are always aware of the present moment after half a second of delay. We live in the past. The present, eliminated from reality along with the past and the future by theoretical physics, is demoted by the experimental data of neuroscience to an inevitable past because of the compressed time, of which one is not aware, employed by the mechanisms of consciousness to perceive it. The compression of time confirms the existence of the present, perceived after the time it takes for the brain to process the stimuli that come from the primary mechanisms of knowledge (visual areas, somatosensory etc.), from the prefrontal areas of reflection and from the emotional system to the mechanisms of consciousness. Libet summed up his contribution to the neurobiology of the time: having demonstrated the substantial, i.e. undoubted, duration of about half a second of uninterrupted nerve activity – which he had called cerebral time-on factor (Libet et al., 1991) – before an experience becomes conscious; and to have shown that that interval is not recorded by consciousness as a delay. "Our findings have shown", wrote Libet, "that the production of a conscious experience involves some unique requirements of neuronal activities and that much cerebral neural activity proceeds without being able to elicit any conscious experience" (Libet, 1993, p. 387). After a lecture by Benjamin Libet in Gothenburg in 1993, a local newspaper headlined: "It's proven: we are always late" (Crane, 2005).

Neuropsychologist Karl Spencer Lashley rightly emphasizes the inherently temporal nature of existence, stressing that without understanding the nervous mechanisms of the ability to process the order, interval, duration of sensor and motor events, it is not possible to understand how the brain processes complex stimuli of the real world (Lashley, 1951). This also applies to animals, which have sophisticated mechanisms not only to feel time but also to distinguish and produce temporal orders (Bueti & Buonomano, 2014). We can feel the time of an empty duration of external events or of interiority, confirming the fact that time is *felt* and not *perceived*. Even if we cannot touch it, smell it or see it, we can understand by virtue of what nervous mechanisms do that the sense of time is a fundamental category of consciousness. Treating time without referring to the nervous mechanisms of consciousness, as physicists and philosophers like, is a desperate undertaking.

The question of what time is is likely to end up in the tautology that time is time, but today, with the data of cognitive neurosciences, approaching the nature and the reality of time is not impossible. Time is an inborn scaffolding of brain mechanisms in which the whole reality, including that of mental life, is inserted.

The sense of time

Time feels like an event of the consciousness of us and of the world. The feeling is created by nervous mechanisms active a priori with reference to the experience of the world and of interiority. We feel time even without perceived mental or external events.

The sense of time is a flexible and variable interweaving of rationality, memory, body sense and affectivity. Despite the central role in existence, the nerve base for interval processing and the sense of duration are still quite conjectural. The sense of time is a variable reality, omnipresent and relatively unforeseeable, as individual as the structure and functioning of each brain are. It is realized in several scales related to the many nervous mechanisms selected because they can process it. A brain injury can temporarily or forever extinguish the sense of time (*timeless life*). Those who know these ill-fated patients have an idea of what life is without a temporal dimension. A short-lived condition that allows us to guess at it is that of the patient who wakes up after a narcosis and asks when the operation will begin or if it is already over, with no idea how long it has lasted. A sense of time is essential because it makes possible the behaviour and survival of all living beings endowed with a nervous system.

Time is the result of a complex nervous organization which, in humans, extends from the prefrontal lobes to the cerebellum. By its extension and by connections with the centres of memory, affectivity and rationality, it is comparable to the mechanisms of language, of which time is one of the pillars. A relevant anatomical and functional relationship exists with the congenital brain mechanisms of the sense of three-dimensional space, in which experience is inserted as it is perceived and transmitted to the mechanisms of consciousness by the sense organs. If we stand in a hurry at a red traffic light, it seems that time never passes. If we are not in a hurry, the passage of time is indifferent. Two hours spent next to a beautiful girl, Einstein is said to have said, seems like two minutes (Ornstein, 1978, p. 104). In cases of normal, short or elongated duration, the nervous mechanisms of the sense of time work differently, communicating to the consciousness a sense of time often determined by emotionality, which becomes a longer or shorter duration in the case of boredom or frenzy. The experience of time is created by the brain – with the sharing of the mechanisms of memory, concentration, reflection, motions and of the sense of space and causality – as well as by the sequence of events (Lake, 2016). Prudence is advisable when assessing the emotional aspect of the sense of time. There is talk of the arrogance of those who are regularly late, if they feel like the lord of their time and of those who await them. This is not always the case: a young patient of mine, after the removal of a benign medium-sized tumour from the right hemisphere of the cerebellum, was no longer able to be punctual due to a defect in the sense of duration. That does not depend on the will but on how the brain (or cerebellum) works (Gibbon et al., 1997).

Conscious experiences of time sense

There are five conscious experiences of time: experience of durability, simultaneity and succession, sequence of events, sense of the present, anticipation of the future (Pöppel, 1978). To these mechanisms must be added a sixth, which marks time during sleep then in unconsciousness. These are different experiences, and therefore their nervous mechanisms are, in part, different too, confirming experimental data according to which a single centre of temporal experience does not exist. It involves different cortical and subcortical areas, common to other experiences, in particular the sense of space and number. The building blocks of the sense of time are the cerebral areas of the memory, in particular the hippocampus, which is the key organ of both the memory and the sense of time. The *verbal forms* "is," "was," "will" indicate different ways of describing time. Time, in its various aspects and despite the various mechanisms that produce it, is a flowing unity, because as such, it is felt by conscience. The various mechanisms of which it is constituted provide the consciousness with unified information. Its various aspects have a common nervous foundation that gives time its teleological nature: both absolute time (GT) and phenomenological time (PT) order life and prevent – as physicist John Archibald Wheeler found written in the graffito of a urinal – that everything happens at the same time (Wheeler, as cited in Carroll, 2010, p. 10).

Duration

We're in the car and we need to turn left. Another vehicle, in the opposite lane, comes towards us. The distance of that vehicle and its speed make us understand whether we have time to turn or if we have to wait for it to pass. The mechanisms of time coordinate the data and provide our consciousness with information about the duration, i.e. whether the time available to turn left is sufficient. We ask ourselves: does the judgment on the duration of an event depend on specialized nerve mechanisms, equipped with particular nerve structures that process and transfer the temporal relationships between events to our consciousness? Or is it the representation of duration intrinsic to the dynamics of the nerve mechanisms inherent in the event (Benini, 2020a)? Duration, like all variants of the sense of time, would depend on the duration of the activation of the network of neurons synchronized in the event (Wittmann, 2013).

The primary visual cortex would produce the sense of the duration of the visual stimulus and acoustic area and the sense of the duration of the sound, without the need to resort to its own and exclusive mechanisms of the sense of time. In this case, the mechanism that transmits the sense of time to the centres of consciousness could process at the same time other, different stimuli. The theory that the sense of time depends on specialized structures and not on the mechanisms of various cognitive activities is more corroborated than the other because of the facility with which we can compare time between different sensory modes: let us think, for example, the subjective duration of an event depends on the attention it arouses. Volunteers are shown, on the screen of a computer, black circles in succession for 10 to 50 milliseconds: the unexpected apparition of a red circle is perceived as longer. The subjective expansion of time is a distortion attributed to the amount of information provided by an event which, because it is unexpected, stimulates more attention. During dangerous events (an accident, a robbery), subjective time flows slower (Tse et al., 2004). If the volunteers know that the appearance of the abnormal signal announces a cash reward, the subjective duration of its presence on the monitor is even longer (Failing & Theeuwes, 2016). The higher the reward, the more attention is given and the longer the duration.

Sleep, insomnia and time

During sleep, the mechanisms of the sense of time are working: self-awakening depends on the level of cortical activation of the mechanisms of the will, which receive information from those of time. It is not a surprising mechanism if we consider that humanity, until a little over a century ago, did not have alarm clocks available to them. Self-awakening was the rule, except for the few who could afford to be woken up by someone else. Evolution has selected the mechanisms of time during sleep and those of self-awakening, without which there would be no hunting and fishing, agriculture, schools, battles, travel, navigation and much of what is part of the cultural evolution with more or less rigorous temporal constraints.

The importance of sleep in the stabilization of memories even in the long term, for example, is a common experience confirmed by many researchers, also in the animal world (Gross, 2019). The consolidation of memories in sleep occurs due to the intense activity of the hippocampus and parahippocampal areas. The significance of sleep for a sense of time is confirmed by insomnia, which leads to a considerable slowing down of the sense of time (Vanable et al., 2000; Miró et al., 2003).

Time compression in advanced age

A particular time compression, probably different also for the mechanisms involved, from the suppression considered up to now, characterizes the advanced age, in which time "goes flying", as the saying goes. Time compression is usually more retrospective than prospective, because in old age, if the days are empty of commitments, often, time never passes. The past is compressed into a time that seems to have passed "in a moment". To which modifications of the cerebral mechanisms of time, which occur in a more or less evident form as a biological form in all brains, this distortion is to be reported, is not known. In circumscribed brain lesions, usually left frontal lobe stroke, it may become impossible to place even important events in the right period. A patient of mine suffering from three frontal strokes on the left over the course of 28 years, in addition to a slight difficulty in finding words, attributed events in the past, such as the high school or graduation exam, described in order and richness of detail, to the last three or four years, even though his 30-year-old daughter born after graduation sat next to him. In the late autumn of his life, the poet Francesco Petrarca traces the experience of the time of his whole life in a few wonderful lines:

> *[. . .] thinking about my life, in which*
> *this morning I was a child and now I am old.*
> *What more than a day is mortal life?*
>   (Petrarca, 1858)

> *Original: "Pensando al viver mio, nel quale stamani ero un*
> *fanciullo e ora sono vecchio. Che più di un giorno è la vita*
> *mortale?"*

With the advancement of age, the sense of time in front of us becomes more important: that is, the future. The past loses its importance. Goals, preferences, attention, memory are changing when the horizon of time shrinks.

Sense of time in animals

The ability of an animal to survive without the mechanisms of temporal and spatial orientation and an elementary numerical capacity (*numerosity*) is unimaginable. Entomologists study the sense of time that contributes to regulating the highly disciplined social organization of bees – beloved and precious insects. An example: if you place food in four places and at four different times, the bees learn to fly at the right time to the right place. Not only that: after the first few trips, they arrive a few moments earlier, probably with the premeditated purpose of anticipating their colleagues (Menzel & Eckoldt, 2016). The mouse is very fond of cheese. To get a good bite, the mouse has two paths; one forces him to stop halfway for a minute, the other, of the same length, keeps him still for six minutes. After the first trips, the mouse carefully avoids the second path (Gibbon, 1977). Laboratory mice, fed once a day always at the same time and in the same place, after a certain time, a few minutes before the arrival of the food, were stopping what they were doing and moving to the place where the food was placed. They demonstrate memory, sense of time, of duration and space (Grondin & Girard, 2005). All these examples and the many others that could be added support the hypothesis that the anticipation of the future is part of the sense of time widespread in human beings and in the animal world (Buonomano, 2017).

Theoretical physics deny the existence of time

No physicist, from Newton onwards, although discussing, arguing, affirming and denying time, has wondered what time is and where it comes from. Many of them deny the existence of time even if what can be measured must be real. The contradiction between neurobiology and physics on the existence of an essential category of life is less and less comprehensible.

Theoretical physicists, with very elegant equations unrelated to reality, deny the existence of time, even if what can be measured must be real. No physicist, from Newton onwards, although discussing, arguing, affirming and denying time, has wondered what time is and where it comes from. Seeing is believing: there is no text on time written by physicists; no book with an explicit title on the birth and history of time questions the nature of time. For the physicist Carlo Rovelli, for instance, common sense would have no reason to be alarmed by the flaking of time, because the time-less world "is clear, windy and full of beauty [. . .] like the arid beauty of chapped lips of teenagers" (Rovelli, 2017, p. 107). The timeless world, rather than resembling the chapped lips of young girls, is meaningless and inconsistent with reality, given that we feel the world as a sequence of events that take place over time. The idea of a timeless reality is staggering, and it is difficult to understand its coherence. Some physicists, however, have now a different opinion. The eminent neuroscientist Lee Smolin (2013) argues that a capital error of physics starting with Einstein is the negation of time.

The reality of time as a nervous mechanism and the sense that animal consciousness and human self-consciousness have, of which time is an essential element, is an evolution of life that no physical equation, however elegant, can eliminate. Time is real, the result of a complex nervous organization which, in humans, extends from the prefrontal lobes to the cerebellum. There is no doubt that the congenital nervous mechanisms of time are a fundamental pylon of human self-consciousness and of the life of living beings with a nervous system.

References

Arntzenius, E. (2012). *Space, Time and Stuff*. Oxford University Press

Benini, A. (2020a). *La durata in neurobiologia del tempo* (Nuova ed.). Cortina

Benini, A. (2020b, February 23). *Hermann von Helmholtz: Così nacque la scienza del sistema nervoso*. Domenicale Sole24Ore

Bolzano, B. (1851/1965). *I paradossi dell'infinito*. Cappelli

Bueti, D. & Buonomano, D. V. (2014). Temporal perceptual learning. *Timing and Time Perception* 2, 261–289.

Buonomano, D. (2017). *Your Brain is a Time Machine: The Neuroscience and Physics of Time*. Norton

Cahan, D. (2018). *Helmholtz: A Life in Science*. University of Chicago Press

Carroll, S. (2010). *From Eternity to Here: The Quest for the Ultimate Theory of Time*. Dutton

Crane, T. (2005). *Ready or Not*. The Times Literary Supplement

Failing, M. & Theeuwes, J. (2016). Reward alters the perception of time. *Cognition* 148, 19–26

Finkelstein, G. (2013). *Emil du Bois-Reymond: Neuroscience, Self, and Society in Nineteenth-Century Germany*. MIT Press

Gibbon, J. (1977). Scalar expectancy theory and Weber's law in animal timing. *Psychological Review* 84, 279–325

Gibbon, J., Malapani, C., Dale, C. L. & Gallistel, C. R. (1997). Toward a neurobiology of temporal cognition: Advances and challenges. *Current Opinion in Neurobiology* 7, 170–184

Grondin, S. & Girard, C. (2005). About hemispheric differences in the processing of temporal intervals. *Brain and Cognition* 58, 125–152

Gross, M. (2019). The reasons of sleep. *Current Biology* 29, 775–777

Hegel, G. W. F. (1975). Kant. In: Kopper, J. & Malter, R. (eds), *Materialien zu Kants "Kritik der reinen Vernunft"*. Suhrkamp

Helmholtz, H. V. (1850a). Messungen über den zeitlichen Verlauf der Zuckung animalischer Muskeln und die Fortpflanzungsgeschwindigkeit der Reizung in den Nerven. *Archiv für Anatomie, Physiologie und wissenschaftliche Medizin*, 276–364

Helmholtz, H. V. (1850c/1895). Über die Fortpflanzungsgeschwindigkeit der Nervenreizung. In: *Wissenschaftliche Abhandlungen* (Vol. 3). Barth, 1–3

Helmholtz, H. V. (1921). Die Tatsache in der Wahrnehmung. In: Hertz, P. & Schlick, M. (eds), *Schriften zur Erkenntnistheorie*. Springer, 109–152

Hume, D. (1739/1975). *Trattato sulla natura umana* (Vol. 1). Laterza, 48–112

Jankélévitch, V. (1980/1987). *Il non-so-che e il quasi niente*. Marietti

Kant, I. (1787/1977). *Kritik der reinen Vernunft* (Vol 1). Zürich: Edit. Ex Libris

Lake, J. I. (2016). Recent advances in understanding emotion-driven temporal distortions. *Current Opinion in Behavioral Sciences* 8, 195–202

Lashley, K. S. (1951). The problem of serial order in behavior. In: Beach, F. A. & Hebb, D. O. (eds), *The Neuropsychology of Lashley*. McGraw-Hill, 112–146

Libet, B. (1993). The neural time factor in perception, volition, and free will. In: Libet, B. (ed), *Neurophysiology of Consciousness: Selected Papers and New Essays*. Birkhäuser, 367–383

Libet, B., Alberts, W. W., Wright, E. W., Delattre, L. D., Levin, G. & Feinstein, B. (1979). Subjective referral of the timing for a conscious sensory experience. *Brain* 102, 193–224

Libet, B., Wright, E. W., Feinstein, B. & Pearl, D. K. (1991). Control of the transition from sensory detection to sensory awareness in man. *Brain* 114, 1731–1757

Menzel, R. & Eckoldt, M. (2016). *Die Intelligenz der Biene: Wie sie denken, planen, fühlen und was wir daraus lernen können*. Knaus

Miró, E., Cano-Lozano, M. C. & Buela-Casal, G. (2003). Time estimation during prolonged sleep deprivation and its relation to activation measures. *Human Factors* 45(1), 148–159

Norton Wise, M. (2018). *Aesthetics, Industry, and Science: Hermann von Helmholtz and the Berlin Physical Society*. University of Chicago Press

Ornstein, R. E. (1978). *La psicologia della coscienza*. Angeli, 104

Petrarca, F. (14th century/1858). *Il Canzoniere di Francesco Petrarca*

Plato. (ca. 360 B.C.E.). *Timaeus*

Pöppel, E. (1978). Time perception. In: Held, R., Leibowitz, H. W. & Teuber, H. L. (eds), *Perception* (Vol. 7). Springer, 713–728

Rovelli, C. (2017). *L'ordine del tempo*. Adelphi, 107

Shanon, B. (2001). Altered temporality. *Journal of Consciousness Studies* 8, 35–58

Smolin, L. (2013). *Time Reborn: From the Crisis in Physics to the Future of the Universe*. Penguin Books

Tse, P. U., Intriligator, J., Rivest, J. & Cavanagh, P. (2004). Attention and the subjective expansion of time. *Perception & Psychophysics* 66, 1171–1189

Vanable, P. A., Aikens, J. E., Tadimeti, L., Caruana-Montaldo, B. & Mendelson, W. B. (2000). Sleep latency and duration estimates among sleep disorder patients. *Sleep* 23(1), 1–9

Wittmann, M. (2013). The inner sense of time: How the brain creates a representation of duration. *Nature Reviews Neuroscience* 14, 217–223

Chapter 4

Discussion of Arnaldo Benini's paper

Neurobiology of time

Katy Bogliatto

Psychoanalysis originated as a scientific model built on the exploration of the unconscious processes of the mind and has remained so while expanding geographically to diverse areas of the world. Sigmund Freud offered a minimalist three-pronged definition, describing psychoanalysis as an investigative procedure, a method of treatment, and a set of theories derived from the two elements (Freud, 1923/1959b). Since those early days, it has thrived with the contribution of many authors: Melanie Klein, Wilfred Bion, Donald Winnicott, Jacques Lacan, Heinz Kohl, André Green, José Bleger, and many others. The result has been the development of a variety of theoretical models and the broadening of clinical practices enriching and adding layers of complexity to the study of the human being within their environment.

In 1900, even as Freud was writing about his discovery of "the royal road to the unconscious", the origin of the psyche was regarded as a product of the evolution of biological forces (Freud, 1911) with drive movements closely anchored to and entangled with the physical body (Freud, 1895). In the previous chapter, Arnaldo Benini invites the reader to view the question of time through the lens of a neuroscientist. The subject of time is deeply connected to the psychoanalyst's field of interest – we conceive of numerous dimensions of experiencing time; this includes the analytic relationship, as well as the individual's development and the construction of subjectivity.

Since the dawn of time itself, the experience of time has been a controversial subject, debated in several fields: philosophical, psychoanalytical, scientific, and socio-cultural. Benini's paper focuses on the bodily grounding of the reality of the sense of time, locating it in the central nervous system in human beings and also in every being with a central

DOI: 10.4324/9781003660118-4

nervous system. Indeed, following Benini's description, the acquisition of the sense of temporality is a fundamental determinant of existence: time structures human experience and is the grid of every cognitive event.

Yet, paradoxically, Benini reminds us that our conscious mode of experiencing the present time – the subjective sense of simultaneity – is "always in the past". Neuroscientific data has demoted our "subjective" consciousness of the present to "the past" as it is consciously perceived with a time gap of 0.5 seconds "after the stimulus has happened". Consciousness has employed the mechanism of "compressed time" to enable the perception of simultaneity.

An intricate and dense network of neuronal connections work together, taking interweaving paths extending from prefrontal lobes to the cerebellum, and involving along the way the hypothalamus and basal ganglia. Their task is to process and connect the complex simultaneity of stimulus and actions with the centres of memory, emotions, and rationality, and this multiplex is intimately related with the mechanisms that generate the sense of three-dimensional space. Our central nervous system processes an infinite volume of information from internal and external stimuli that are part of our everyday life; we experience the result as language, thought, memory, body sensations, emotions, and the components that build an individual mode of understanding objective reality and causality.

Time, space, and causality are intimately related and are the end result of complex neuronal networks that produce the sense of time. Benini describes how these processes take place in various central neural zones, leading to five conscious experiences of time; this is in addition to the important process that takes place during sleep, working closely with memory consolidation. They all build the experience of flowing unity, the capacity to live, understand, move in the environment, and interact with others.

I also entered and read Benini's paper from a psychoanalytic vertex, in a free state of mind, and as in a daydream, "without memory, desire or understanding" (Bion, 1970). I wondered what kind of psychic traces could be left by these gaps of 0.5 seconds, which B. Libet et al. (1979) has called "retroactive referral time"; how would it link with our psychoanalytic model of the mind, which maps zones of functioning ranging from the undifferentiated unconscious mode to more conscious reasoning and thinking?

Given the belief that the origin of our psychic life is undifferentiated as in the newborn baby, and earlier, in the in-utero baby at the end of pregnancy; and that following Bion, the mother or caregiver's α-dreaming capacity is needed to contain it; and further, taking into account the neuroplasticity of the infant, what status should be given to the sensorial, non-symbolised traces contained in the 0.5 seconds of retroactive referral time? Could these add up during an individual's lifespan? Could the adding up of these unconscious sensorial traces linked to unconscious temporal mechanisms be considering an underground spring flowing and feeding the unconscious flow throughout the life of the individual? Perhaps this connects with the psychoanalytic process, and we might imagine linking the "thoughts that are not yet thought" (Bion, 1977/1989), the more primitive mental states, with the unconscious traces that have been left or lost in the interweaving path of the myriad neural connections.

Benini's paper and other neuroscientific understanding (Damasio, 1994; Gallese et al., 1996) reveal the connection between emotions and thinking taking place in a complex network linking prefrontal cortex zones to more primitive critical zones such as the basal brain and then the more conscious zones of the brain. Emotions influence neuronal mechanisms, leading to rationality, learning, memory and understanding of causality.

The individual needs the other to thrive; in order to live, interaction with others is essential. The presence of a good-enough balance of presence and absence of the object is needed to transform sensoriality and emotions, and it enables the development of what Bion called the α-function. This is the foundation for the development of a sense of Self, the capacity to symbolise, think, and give sense to experience, relationship, and life (Winnicott, 1971; Bion, 1962; Milner, 1957) – in short, the fundamental necessities for humankind to live.

The sense of temporality is a fundamental parameter in psychoanalysis. Omnipresent even if not explicitly named, it makes possible the elaboration of internal and external subjective representation of the experiences linked to life and closely related to objective reality.

Or perhaps, in reading Benini's paper, I lost myself in some conjectural, naïve, and simplistic thoughts . . . . In a dream that led me, like Borges's (1962/1967) hero, to experience the ineffable, to find and see the Aleph in Carlos Argentino's cellar, where all the points, all the places of space converge, in a space-time navel.

References

Bion, W. R. (1962/1967). A theory of thinking. In: *Second Thoughts*. New York: Jason Aronson

Bion, W. R. (1970/1986). *Attention and Interpretation*. London: Karnac

Bion, W. R. (1977/1989). *Two Papers: The Grid and the Caesura*. London: Karnac

Borges, J. L. (1962/1967). *L'Aleph. L'imaginaire*. Gallimard

Damasio, A. R. (1994/2010). *L'erreur de Descartes*. Ed. Odile Jacob, Sciences

Freud, S. (1895). Project for a scientific psychology. *SE* 1, 281–397

Freud, S. (1900). The interpretation of dreams. *SE*, 4–5

Freud, S. (1911). Formulations on the two principles of mental functioning. *SE* 12, 218–226

Freud, S. (1923/1959b). Two encyclopaedia articles. *SE* 18, 235–259

Gallese, V. et al. (1996, April). Action recognition in the premotor cortex. *Brain*. Apr; 119, 596–609. https://pubmed.ncbi.nlm.nih.gov/8800951/

Libet, B., Alberts, W. W., Wright, E. W., Delattre, L. D., Levin, G. & Feinstein, B. (1979). Subjective referral of the timing for a conscious sensory experience. *Brain* 102, 193–224

Milner, M. (1957). *On Not Being Able to Paint*. London: Heinemann

Winnicott, D. W. (1971). *Playing and Reality*. New York: Basic Books

Chapter 5

What is time? – Thoughts of a physicist

Gernot Münster

Introduction

The notion of time plays a fundamental role in human experience, think-ing, and feeling. Our image of the world is inconceivable without the con-cept of time. So what is time?

With this question, the sixth chapter of Thomas Mann's "The Magic Mountain" begins:

> What is time? A mystery – insubstantial and almighty. A prerequisite of the world of appearances, a motion, coupled and mingled with the being of bodies in space and their movement. But would there be no time, if there were no motion? No motion if no time? Just ask! Is time a function of space? Or the other way around? Or are both identical? Go ahead, ask!
>
> (Mann, 2002, p. 365)

For a physicist, time is a concept of prime importance. So let us ask about the nature of time. This, however, is more a question for philoso-phers. Not being a philosopher, allow me to skate on thin ice for a moment. In the literature, you find quite different answers. According to Wittgen-stein (1970), "What is time?" is not a meaningful question but a mislead-ing one. "Time" is not the name of an object. On the other hand, Kant gives an answer in his transcendental philosophy: according to him, time is a pure form of sensible intuition (*reine Form der Anschauung*). "Time is a necessary representation that grounds all intuitions. In regard to appear-ances in general one cannot remove time, though one can very well take the appearances away from time. Time is therefore given *a priori*. In it alone is all actuality of appearances possible" (Kant, 1781/1998, p. 162).

DOI: 10.4324/9781003660118-5

Natural scientists often express themselves in a more casual way. The physicist John A. Wheeler, the Ph.D. adviser of Richard Feynman, liked to characterise time in the way he found it in a graffito in the men's room of the Pecan Street Cafe in Austin, Texas, in 1976: "Time is nature's way to keep everything from happening all at once" (Wheeler, 1994, p. 1).

The phenomenon of time leads to a number of interesting questions: Does time have a beginning or an end? Is "time travel" possible? Can time cyclically close in a circle? How does the difference between past and future come about? Which of these questions can be answered by physics?

A distinction concerning the concept of time, which is often discussed in the philosophical literature about time, has been made by the Cambridge philosopher J. M. E. McTaggart (1908). He introduced the notions of A-series and B-series for the temporal ordering of events. In the A-series, events are divided into those belonging to the past, to the present, and to the future. The classification continuously changes: events are first in the future, then in the present, and finally remain in the past. Time is, of course, ordered in the A-series: for each pair of unequal times, t_1 and t_2, either t_1 is earlier than t_2 or vice versa. The A-series allows tensed propositions, like "we had a reception yesterday evening". In the B-series, temporal positions are just linearly ordered with the earlier/later relation. It does not make use of the notions of past, present, and future. Only tenseless propositions, like "we had a reception in the evening of April 8th" are possible in the B-series. The most significant difference between the two series is the fact that in the A-series, there is a "now", whereas this concept is missing in the B-series. In the philosophy of time, those who consider the A-series or the B-series to be more fundamental are called A-theorists or B-theorists, respectively. Philosophers discuss whether future and past are real or whether they exist, and they debate about the status of the present (Le Poidevin, 1998). We shall, however, not delve into these metaphysical questions here.

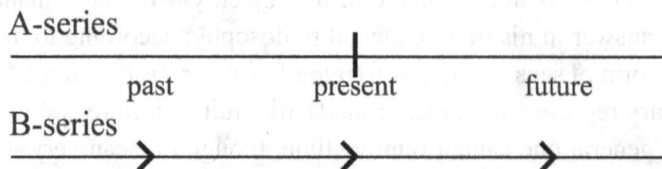

Figure 5.1 McTaggart's A-series and B-series.

Time, the experience of time, and the measurement of time have philosophical, biological, physiological, psychological, sociological, and physical aspects, which are viewed differently in the different disciplines. For example, in physiology, the subjectively experienced "moment" (the critical time interval T_c) covers a period of about 30 msec, and the "subjective presence" (the mental presence time T_p) has a duration of several seconds (Grüsser, 1989; Pöppel, 1989), while in physics, the presence is understood as the sharp boundary between past and future.

In the following, we shall deal with a few aspects of time in the context of physics.

Time in physics

Einstein is said to have answered the question asked at the beginning of this paper with: "Time is what the clock shows." What at first glance seems like a flippant answer is, in fact, an expression of his years of struggle over the fundamentals of space and time. The operational approach to time, reflected in the quote, was the key to setting up the theory of relativity. The associated success and progress in understanding time are based on a retreat, a simplification, in that within the framework of physics, the subjective elements are disregarded, and we content ourselves with the measurable. This notion of time, measured by clocks, is called "physical time" or "objective time".

On the other hand, there is "phenomenological time" or "subjective time", which is the time that we see passing in our individual experience. Depending on our particular state of being, phenomenological time might appear to run faster or slower than physical time. Also, our experience of events and processes includes the modal structure of time, corresponding to the A-series, with its past, present, and future.

In contrast to that, physics does not know the "now". Why is this so? In general, physics is not interested in single events or processes. It is not interested in the fall of Newton's apple or of my teacup. Instead, it is interested in regularities, which it tries to describe in terms of laws, e.g. Galileo's law of falling bodies. Such a law is supposed to be valid (within its scope of application and within a certain precision) universally and at all times. Therefore, references to singular points in time, and in particular to the "now", are not admitted in physical laws. It should be mentioned that in exceptional cases reference to particular dates is made in physics, like in astrophysics, where, for example, the detection of gravitational waves on 14th September 2015 and Tycho Brahe's supernova of 11th November 1572 are considered. Nevertheless, these dates are referred to in a tenseless way. So, in general, physical statements about temporal instances are made according to the B-series.

Are physical time and phenomenological time in contradiction to each other? Are the A-series and B-series incompatible? I do not think so. Every account of temporal processes or events has its origin in human perception. Expressing experiences in terms of phenomenological time or physical time, using the A-series or the B-series, means to employ different representations of the same reality. Objective time is obtained by an abstraction of subjective time based on an intersubjective agreement about the meaning of clocks.

Measurement of time

Time, more precisely time intervals, is measured with clocks. What is a clock? Clocks are characterised by periodic processes that are used to define periods of time. In the course of history, time measurement developed from the rotation of the earth to water clocks and wheel clocks to more modern technical constructs. A milestone was the chronograph by John Harrison from 1759. The development continued to today's quartz clocks and atomic clocks. The precision of the currently available atomic clocks has given rise to the valid definition of the fundamental unit of time by means of atomic processes: One second corresponds to 9,192,632,770 periods of the radiation emitted by the transition between the two hyperfine levels of the ground state of atoms of caesium 133.

Is not a vicious circle lurking here? Is not the definition of time units via periodic processes, whose uniformity is assumed, circular? Would not the old definitions of the hour and the second via the rotation of the earth be just as viable as the one using modern atomic clocks? In this spirit, Percy W. Bridgman (1882–1961), winner of the 1946 Nobel Prize in physics, proposed to define physical concepts and units in an operational way (Bridgman, 1927). The meaning of a scientific term would then be given by a specific measurement method. Consequently, there would be different seconds: an "earth second", a "quartz clock second", a "caesium clock second", etc. When I was young, I read in a newspaper about the – at that time – most accurate atomic clock. Its precision was also specified, and

I wondered how it could have been determined if no more accurate clock existed for comparison. Indeed, in the operational framework, it would not make sense to ask for the precision of an atomic clock if time units are defined by means of this clock.

The actual meaning of time and definition of time units in physics is, however, different. The concept of time is theory-laden. It does not have its meaning by virtue of any particular periodic process, which is defined to be uniform, but within an entire system of description of nature, which should be consistent in itself and simple. The laws of physics contain time as a parameter, often denoted t. For example, in Newtonian mechanics, the motion of a free particle is described by the equation of motion $\ddot{x} = 0$ and its solution $x(t) = vt$, where v is the velocity. The time parameter t is involved in the laws of electrodynamics, relativity, quantum theory, etc. It is a theoretical term that finds its meaning within the framework of a theoretical description of a domain of phenomena. It is specified in such a way that the laws of physics take a simple form. Imagine, for example, that by contrast, t would be defined in terms of the rotation of the earth. This would be logically possible, but in this case, the motion of a free particle would not be uniform, and the various laws of physics would take rather complicated and impractical forms, since the rotation of the earth is not uniform with respect to these other phenomena. Instead, time is an idealised concept, which is tied to the phenomena and experiments by means of models, idealisations, and bridge principles. Time intervals and units are then best represented by clocks that currently run most uniform according to their physical description.

Time's arrow

The term "arrow of time" means the fact that time has an inherent direction that distinguishes the past from the future. It becomes apparent in our experience in everyday life and in the sciences. The directionality of time has been put into words very nicely by Friedrich Schiller in his *Proverbs of Confucius*:

> *Threefold is the march of time:*
> *While the future slow advances,*
> *Like a dart the present glances,*
> *Silent stands the past sublime.*
> (Schiller, 1851, p. 259)

C.F. von Weizsäcker (1971) has summed up this fact in the succinct statement "the past is factual, the future is possible." This structure of time appears to be inextricably linked to the concept of time. Why is that? Kant again had a deep insight into this. In our lives, we constantly have experiences. Gaining experience, however, means learning from the past for the future. So this structure of time, the difference between past and future, is a necessary condition for the possibility of experience.

Physics is an empirical science; it is based on experience. The arrow of time is thus a prerequisite for physics. Therefore, at first glance, it appears reasonable to assume that physics cannot justify the arrow of time. Is that really the case? I do not think so. The circle that arises when physics searches for a physical reason for the arrow of time does not have to be vicious. It is a matter of semantic consistency whether the physical justification for the arrow of time, expressed in the language of physics, and the arrow of time as a prerequisite for physics fit together. So let us turn to the issue of an eventual physical justification for time's arrow. There is a lot of literature about this, but I will only mention the books of Halliwell et al. (1994), Zeh (1992), and Davies (1974).

The fundamental laws of physics that describe particles and their interactions are time-reversible (with the exception of CP violation in the weak interactions of elementary particles, which is not relevant here). Each process may also run backwards in time. But the processes taking place in nature are obviously not time-reversible: a cup that falls to the ground shatters into many pieces; the reverse process has never been observed. How does that come about? Where does this arrow of time come from, which does not originate from the fundamental laws of nature?

On closer inspection, one can distinguish several arrows of time:

1. Psychological: our memory is directed towards the past and not towards the future,
2. Thermodynamic: according to the second law of thermodynamics, entropy always increases (I leave out the details and necessary prerequisites for this law here),
3. Electrodynamic: radiation propagates outwards from the source as time progresses and does not flow in concentrically,
4. Quantum theoretical: the changes of state in the measurement process of a quantum system are irreversible, and
5. Cosmological: the universe is expanding.

Detailed inspection shows that the time's arrows 1 to 4 are connected to each other. The irreversible processes associated with them take place on the basis of probability laws, which describe a progression from ordered to more disordered states. Thereby, the overall disorder of the systems under consideration increases. Counterintuitive as it might appear, this also applies to our memories. To remember some event means that it has left traces in our memory, which are realised by certain neuronal structures. Traces in general represent remnants of irreversible processes, which are accompanied by an increase of the total disorder (entropy).

In physics, entropy is a measure of the disorder of a system. The time arrow can then be traced back to the fact that an ordered initial state (with low entropy) has been present. While the laws are time-reversible, the initial conditions lead to irreversibility of processes. The question of time's arrow therefore leads to the question of the origin of the ordered initial state. There is still no generally accepted answer to this, but there is a plausible hypothesis that the origin is based in cosmology, and the expansion of the universe acts as a kind of "master arrow of time".

A remark is in order here. On Earth, we often observe the emergence of ordered structures in apparent contradiction to the increase in disorder (entropy). This contradiction is illusory: in open systems, complexity can grow locally at the expense of disorder in the outside world (Prigogine, 1977). Evolution does not conflict with thermodynamics.

Theory of relativity

It is not possible for a physicist to talk about time without taking the theory of relativity into account. It was established in one of the five famous works from Einstein's "annus mirabilis", 1905, entitled *"Zur Elektrodynamik bewegter Körper"* ("On the Electrodynamics of Moving Bodies"). The title sounds inconspicuous and rather technical. But this work is about the very nature of space and time. In it, Einstein overthrows concepts of space and time that had been thousands of years old.

Difficulties in electrodynamics and optics led Einstein to investigate the fundamentals of the concepts of space and time. From 1902 to 1909, he worked in the patent office in Bern. He wrote to his friend Conrad Habicht: "After eight working hours there are still eight hours for miscellaneous, and a whole Sunday" (Einstein, 1905, p. 32). The result of this was the theory of relativity, which brought with it a radical new way of thinking about space and time. Consequences of the theory are:

1. Relativity of simultaneity,
2. Relativity of time,
3. Relativity of lengths.

Let me make a few remarks about the relativity of time. What is meant with that? The passage of time, more precisely the running of clocks, depends on how the observer and the clock move relative to each other. A clock moving at a certain speed relative to us runs slower than a clock at rest. So does running keep you young? Well, the effect is extremely small for ordinary speeds. The factor by which the moving clock of a cyclist slows down is 1.00000000000000017, which is equivalent to 1 second in 200 million years. Only at speeds comparable to the speed of light of 299,792.458 km/sec does the effect become significant. At 90% of the speed of light, the factor is 2.3, and at 99% of the speed of light, it is already 7.1.

It is important that not only artificial clocks are affected but all processes, including biological ones. It is time itself, the passing of which is relative. The relativity of time is often illustrated by the so-called twin paradox: a twin leaves earth in a spaceship, which travels into space at high speed and returns several years later. While the twin who remained on Earth has aged to an old man, his much-less-aged sister climbs out of the spaceship. Although the realisation of this story is far beyond today's possibilities, the effect has been confirmed experimentally with the help of atomic clocks in airplanes.

The effects resulting from the theory of relativity are by no means esoteric fantasies of scientists but play a role in many areas of today's physics and technology. An example is the GPS (global positioning system). Without taking into account the theory of relativity, an error of 10 km would add up in the GPS devices every day, and some of you would have missed today's venue by a long way!

Simultaneity

The relativity of simultaneity is a consequence of the theory of relativity, which is of crucial significance for our understanding of time. Surprisingly, it has received rather little attention among philosophers. Exceptions

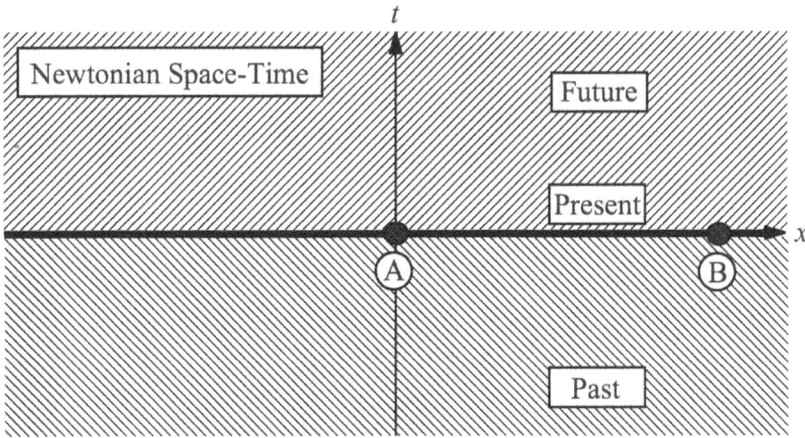

Figure 5.2 Newtonian space-time. Shown are the time axis and one spatial axis. The global present is indicated by a thick horizontal line.

are, for example, H. Putnam (1964) and Wüthrich (2013) and works cited therein.

In physics before Einstein, the idea of an absolute time prevailed, which is equally universally valid and measurable for every observer. In his "*Philosophiae Naturalis Principia Mathematica*" from 1687, Newton writes: "Absolute, true, and mathematical time, of itself, and from its own nature, flows equably without relation to anything external." Absolute time implies that a concept of global simultaneity is possible. If, in Newtonian space-time, an event A takes place at a certain location x_A and time t_A, then an event B, happening at any other location at the same time t_A, is simultaneous with A. The existence of an absolute notion of simultaneity allows to define the concepts of future, present, and past unambiguously; see Figure 5.2. What is now for me here is now for everybody elsewhere.

The relativistic situation is substantially different from the Newtonian one. The geometry of space-time is represented by the so-called Minkowski space; see Figure 5.3.

The global past and future of an event A in Newtonian space-time are now replaced by two regions called "causal past" and "causal future", depending on A. (Choosing $x_A = 0$ and $t_A = 0$ for simplicity, they are specified by the conditions $t \leq -|x|/c$ and $t \geq +|x|/c$, respectively, where c is the speed of light.) The Newtonian present of A has become a whole region of

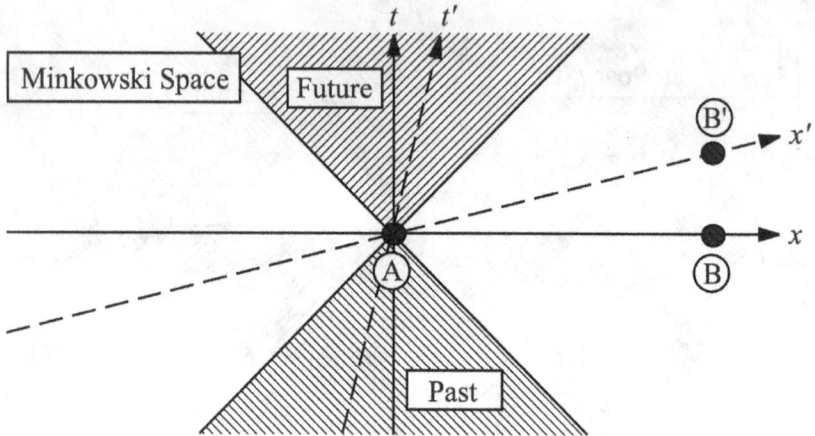

Figure 5.3 Minkowski space. Shown are the time axis and one spatial axis. Note that for better visibility of relativistic effects, units are chosen such that propagation of light takes place on diagonal lines. So if 1 cm on the *t*-axis corresponds to 1 sec, then 1 cm on the *x*-axis corresponds to 300.000 km. Causal past and causal future are abbreviated as past and future. Depending on the velocity of an observer at A, events B or B′ are Einstein-simultaneous with A.

space-time between past and future, the points in it being called space-like relative to A.

Which points in Minkowski space are simultaneous with A? Consider the following situation in Figure 5.3. Physicist Bob works in a distant laboratory. At a certain time, he is looking for the result of a quantum physical experiment. This event is denoted B. Let us assume that the result of the experiment is not predetermined. For Bob, its outcome is open before B and factual afterwards. At point A, philosopher Alice wonders how the experiment of physicist Bob went. For her, the question is whether event B has already taken place or not. That amounts to the question of simultaneity of A and B.

Looking at Figure 5.3, it seems as if A and B are simultaneous. But Einstein's revolutionary insight was that there is no unambiguous concept of simultaneity. As he showed, one can indeed define a kind of simultaneity, called "Einstein-simultaneity", which, however, depends on the velocity of the observer A and is thus a relative notion. I refer to Einstein's (2001) beautiful book *Relativity: The Special and the General Theory*, where he explains these issues in a generally understandable way by means of moving trains. If the *x*- and *t*-axes in Figure 5.3 correspond to the rest frame of

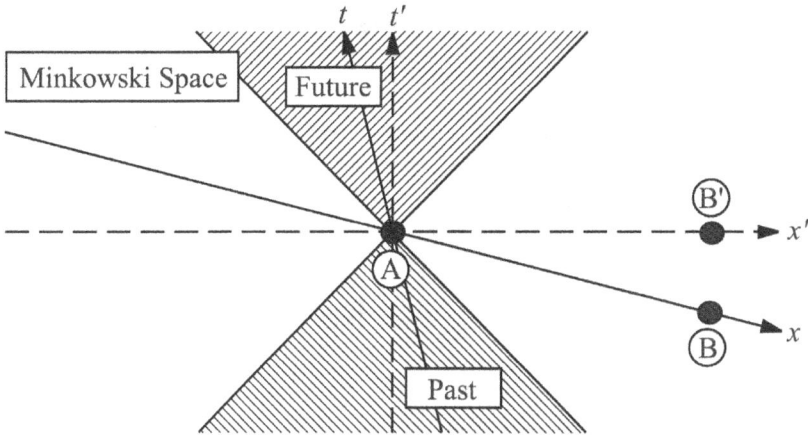

Figure 5.4 Minkowski space. The same situation as in Figure 5.3 is drawn differently but equivalently.

Alice, then the points on the x-axis, including B, are Einstein-simultaneous to A. As mentioned, this notion depends on the motion of Alice. If she walks through her office, her rest frame is represented by the x'- and t'-axes, obtained from the previous coordinates by a Lorentz transformation. (For better visibility, the angles are exaggerated in the figure.) The event in Bob's laboratory, which is Einstein-simultaneous to A, is now indicated by B'. In everyday situations, the difference will be extremely small. But for the sake of principle, consider Bob's laboratory to be located in the Andromeda galaxy. If Alice moves with 3 km/s towards him, the event B' is later than B by a considerable amount of 9 days.

A remark is in order. Figure 5.3 might suggest that the x-t-frame is privileged because of the $90°$ angle between its axes. But this is an optical illusion. This orthogonality does not have a meaning in Minkowski geometry. The same situation can be displayed in an equivalent manner as in Figure 5.4.

We have to see that for events at Bob's place, being simultaneous with event A does not have an inherent meaning. So we have to realise that there is no unambiguous way for Alice to consider one of Bob's times as "now" simultaneous with her "now".

The inevitable conclusion of this consideration is that for Alice, now thinking about Bob's experiment, there is no way to give a meaning to statements about its status of being completed or being still open. This is a severe challenge for our understanding of reality and for A-theorists in particular. I consider this to be the most serious problem in the philosophy of time.

Einstein appears to have been aware of the consequences of the relativity of simultaneity. He probably arrived at a deterministic worldview, in which there is no room for an open future. Shortly before his death in 1955, in a letter to the family of his deceased friend Michele Besso, he wrote, "For us believing physicists, the distinction between past, present and future only has the meaning of an illusion, though a stubborn one" (Einstein, 1972, pp. 537–538).

References

Bridgman, P. W. (1927). *The Logic of Modern Physics*. Macmillan

Davies, P. C. W. (1974). *The Physics of Time Asymmetry*. University of California Press

Einstein, A. (1905/1944). Letter to Conrad Habicht. In: Klein, M. J., Kox, A. J. & Schulmann, R. (eds), *The Collected Papers of Albert Einstein. Vol. 5: The Swiss Years: Correspondence, 1902–1914*. Princeton University Press

Einstein, A. (1917/2001). *Relativity: The Special and the General Theory*. Dover Publications

Einstein, A. (1955/1972). Letter to Vero and Beatrice Besso. In: Speziali, P. (ed), *Albert Einstein – Michele Besso: Correspondance 1903–1955*. Hermann

Grüsser, O.-J. (1989). Zeit und Gehirn. In: Gumin, H. & Meier, H. (eds), *Die Zeit – Dauer und Augenblick*. Piper Verlag, 79–132

Halliwell, J. J., Pérez-Mercader, J. & Zurek, W. H. (eds). (1994). *Physical Origins of Time Asymmetry*. Cambridge University Press

Kant, I. (1781/1998). *Critique of Pure Reason* (Guyer, P. & Wood, A. W., trans). Cambridge University Press

Le Poidevin, R. (ed). (1998). *Questions of Time and Tense*. Clarendon Press

Mann, T. (2002). *Der Zauberberg*. S. Fischer Verlag, quotation translated by G. Münster

McTaggart, J. M. E. (1908). The unreality of time. *Mind* 17(68), 457–474

Pöppel, E. (1989). Erlebte Zeit und die Zeit überhaupt. In: Gumin, H. & Meier, H. (eds), *Die Zeit – Dauer und Augenblick*. Piper Verlag, 369–382

Prigogine, I. (1977). Time, structure and fluctuations. *Nobel Lecture*. https://www.nobelprize.org/prizes/chemistry/1977/prigogine/lecture/

Putnam, H. (1964). Time and physical geometry. *The Journal of Philosophy* 64(8), 240–247

Schiller, F. (1851). Proverbs of Confucius. In Bowring, E. A. (trans), *The Poems of Schiller, Complete: Including All His Early Suppressed Pieces*. John W. Parker & Son. (Original work published in German)

Weizsäcker, C. F. V. (1971). *Die Einheit der Natur*. Carl Hanser Verlag

Wheeler, J. A. (1994). Time today. In: Halliwell, J. J., Pérez-Mercader, J. & Zurek, W. H. (eds), *Physical Origins of Time Asymmetry*. Cambridge University Press, 1–29

Wittgenstein, L. (1970). *Das blaue Buch: Eine philosophische Betrachtung.* Suhrkamp Verlag

Wüthrich, C. (2013). The fate of presentism in modern physics. In: Ciuni, R., Miller, K. & Torrengo, G. (eds), *New Papers on the Present – Focus on Presentism*. Philosophia Verlag, 91–131

Zeh, H. D. (1992). *The Physical Basis of the Direction of Time.* Springer

Chapter 6

Discussion of Gernot Münster's paper

What is time? – Thoughts of a physicist

Charlotta Björklind

Reflections after reading 'What is time? – Thoughts of a physicist' by Gernot Münster

It is a rare privilege for a psychoanalyst to be invited to comment on a paper on physics, and as discussant to Gernot Münster's contribution to the EPF Symposium on Time 2022, I will at least give this daunting task a try. It is only made possible by Münster's elegant way of writing for a wider audience, in such a way as to make the layman reader feel welcome into this abstract field and – seductively, perhaps – slightly more intelligent than what is probably merited.

From a psychoanalytical perspective, it is especially fascinating to understand more about a physicist's conceptualization of time – and to explore how (or if at all) the concept of time in external reality relates to the subjective experience and understanding of time. My comments will simply follow my free associations reading Münster's account, which will inevitably and repeatedly direct me into the more familiar terrain of psychoanalysis.

My starting point is precisely this: the physicist explores the fundamental properties and laws that govern space, time, energy, and matter. Physics is the academic study of the laws of *external reality*. Sigmund Freud sought to describe the workings of the mind from a similar perspective, trying to explore and define the fundamental and universal laws that govern the workings of *psychic reality*. Psychoanalytic theory could indeed be described as the systematic study of the similarities and differences between external and internal reality – and psychoanalytic treatment could be defined as a talking cure aimed at assisting the analysand in handling the nearly impossible predicament of existing in these two fundamentally incompatible domains.

DOI: 10.4324/9781003660118-6

Early on in his text, Münster quotes Wheeler, stating that "time is nature's way of keeping everything from happening all at once". This would seem to be a very important psychological function as well. Experiencing everything as happening all at once sounds like a terrifying state of madness. In psychoanalysis, the establishment of the secondary process is what structures our perception and makes a chronological experience possible. This capacity is strongly associated with the acquisition of language and thus fundamentally relational – bound to the capacity to relate to the other as a separate individual, someone *not* bound to one's own psychic reality. The other existing in external reality, apart from myself. However, it is important to note that this ability is exactly that – a *secondary* ability. It is thus not one of the universal laws that govern psychic reality from the start; quite the contrary. The core of the mind, the Unconscious, works through primary process – where everything does, in fact, happen at once. In this universe, there is no gap between the wish and its fulfilment, no negation, no lack, no frustration. Therefore, we often say that there is no (sense of) time in the Unconscious. Perhaps we will return to this.

However, psychoanalysis emphasizes how this establishment of secondary process is essential for survival. Over time (sic!), the body/bodily ego cannot avoid experiencing frustration and lack, and thus, the psyche is forced to develop from this initial state of mere wish and hallucination. New, secondary governing principles are established, expanding our reality, much like the evolvement of the universe after the initial state of extreme density and temperatures of the big bang. Secondary process is hence also what makes possible an (at least) semi-stable link between internal and external reality, thus what keeps us alive. As bodies in the real (world), we need a capacity to adapt to the reality principle, or else we die of starvation or deprivation. Following the rudimentary establishment of secondary process thinking and (partial) acceptance of the reality principle, we manage survival, but we are also forever condemned to a divided existence between two incompatible realities – characterized very much by their respective relations to time.

Münster goes on to explain the model put forth by Cambridge philosopher McTaggart, about the difference between the so-called A- and B-series ordering of temporal events. The A-series divides events into the categories of past, present, and future, whereas the B-series orders events linearly on a chronological timeline, with only an earlier/later relation and no specification of a 'now'. Münster describes how philosophers have argued for the A- and B-theory respectively, in discussing "whether future and past are real, or whether they exist, and they debate the status of the present" (p. 2). He also mentions that physiologists have been able to measure the human subjective experience of the present as a function of the brain.[1] Apparently, the experience of the moment 'now' is 30 msec long. He then goes on to physics, stating that in this discipline devoted to the study of external, objective reality, there is no interest or need of a concept of 'now'. "Physics is not interested in single events or processes" (p. 3)

To reiterate, the present tense exists only in narrative A. If we categorize events accordingly, they continuously move from category future to present to past – for instance, if you are standing on the sidewalk, waiting for someone to pick you up in a car. You watch it approach, the picking-up is still in the future. It stops, and you are presently being picked up. You drive away together, and the event is in the past. But in the B-series, there is only chronological order, no 'now'. In contemporary psychoanalysis, we often oscillate between working in the B-series – that is, by assisting the analysand in constructing a comprehensive, personal historical narrative, ordering events in chronological order – and working in the A-series, i.e. interpreting the enactment of the intrapsychic (somehow linked to a past) in the here and now of the transference. Here, the psychoanalyst thus encounters a paradox. We try (with the effort of our conscious mind) to describe the realm of the Unconscious, establishing the fact that there, we have no dimension of time. Events are not ordered. In fact, there is no distinction between wishes and external events, between memories of 'actual' events and /ph/fantasies of said events. If there is no acknowledgment of frustration, of the external gap between desire and its gratification, there is no unit of time.[2]

The incompatible divide between external and psychic reality is further illustrated by the statement that physics is not interested in single events or processes. Psychoanalysts are, in the end, *only* interested in single events and processes, although we strive to generalize that which can be seen as universal. While we know from clinical experience how the analysand's sense of the present is universally and perpetually overshadowed[3] and intermingled by /fantasies of/ the past, and furthermore, how our imaginations of the future are inescapably steeped in the form of phantasms of breakdowns already /un/experienced,[4] how these dynamics play out is always a unique and singular affair.

All of this, however, is necessarily metaphorical and a rough description at that. In stating that there is no sense of time in the Unconscious, we are speaking from the timed realm of the conscious mind, again always trying to bridge an unbridgeable gap. And paradoxically, the psychoanalyst can only access this timeless Unconscious *in the present* – in fact, this is true for all of us. The timeless, events-happening-all-at-once Unconscious can only briefly make itself known in manifestations in the present tense. Only in the parapraxis, in the enactment, in the mise-en-scène of the ongoing, that which is continuously happening in the Unconscious is temporarily embodied or realized. For a brief moment /in time/, we can catch a glimpse of this timeless event. In the here and now of the transference,[5] in the actuality of the dream – which can only ever be caught après coup – and in the repetition compulsion.[6] We can try to catch the moment in passing, describe it in words, domesticate it into secondary process and (vainly) attempt to pause the present to capture the past/timeless/repressed/unconscious – that of which we know nothing, except how its gravity affects us indirectly.[7] Like the denseness of the black hole, affecting space around it and pulling celestial bodies over the event horizon.

Münster shows how the present only exists in subjective experience, but for us, this (illusion of a) now is the only actual opening to the timelessness of psychic reality – and to the possibility of studying the universal laws governing this other reality.

Münster also refers to Einstein, who famously stated that "Time is what the clock shows." This, of course, brings the crucial role of time in the psychoanalytic setting to mind, where in fact time is what *the analyst's clock shows*.[8] I will not write at length about this. Suffice it to say that through this temporal parameter, we enforce the reality principle within the treatment, contrasting it with the possible workings of the pleasure principle /and its inhibitions/ within the session. We frame the timelessness of the dynamics of the transference with the strict adherence to the limits of external reality, through the time limitation. Again, at best, this can provide a link between psychic and external reality or at least a possibility for the analytic couple to work on that link.

In the second half of his paper, Münster introduces the work of Einstein and the but century-old insight that time is in fact not an absolute but relative to the parameters of space and velocity. He also describes how this shift from understanding time as an absolute parameter, "universally valid and measurable for every observer" (p. 8), overthrows our understanding of the possibility of absolute simultaneity. The similarities with the relativity of time in psychic reality are quite salient – we all have abundant experience of how time seems relative; relative to our state of mind, to our ego functioning, to our containing function – but again, we must be careful of speculating too much about manifest similarities. These are only analogies, not evidence of actual likeness. They should not be taken to prove any similarities between the workings of the (external) universe and the workings of our internal world. In fact, the whole point is that psychic reality is *fundamentally alien* to external reality, and they cannot be compared in any comprehensive manner. Nonetheless, the theoretical models described by Münster led me to associate psychoanalytic understanding of the human capacity of relating to others and how psychoanalysis shows the difficulty involved for us to achieve a mature understanding of inter-relational simultaneity. To borrow a Kleinian perspective, one could state that it takes tremendous and arduous psychic work – of painstaking integration of love and hate, of difficult mourning of the loss of the illusion of omnipotence and control /of the love object/ – for the individual to develop the capacity for love, guilt, and reparation.[9] Only after hard and perilous work, dependent as well on the luck of good-enough circumstances, can we ever hope to establish an outlook of the world in which we appreciate both the otherness and the likeness of the other. Realizing that my friend has a psychic reality of his own may sound cognitively simple but is emotionally extremely difficult. To take in that, at any given moment, more than 8 billion other people exist on this planet with me – with their own passions, struggles, dilemmas, and needs – is all but impossible. At best, perhaps I can achieve enough object constancy, enough theory of mind, to take in the person next to me in the room. For a psychoanalyst, too, then, simultaneity is rendered impossible by the relativity of time and space.

It seems appropriate to end by reflecting on the arrow of time, as it – for the individual subject – without the possibility of exception, points to the end. Münster explains:

The fundamental laws of physics that describe particles and their inter-actions are time- reversible. Each process may also run backwards in time. But the processes taking place in nature are obviously not time-reversible: a cup that falls to the ground shatters into many pieces; the reverse process has never been observed. How does that come about?

Where does this arrow of time come from, which does not originate from the fundamental laws of nature? (1) On closer inspection, one can distinguish several arrows of time: psychological: our memory is directed towards the past and not towards the future, (2) thermo-dynamic: according to the second law of thermodynamics, entropy always increases (I leave out the details and necessary prerequisites for this law here), (3) electrodynamic: radiation propagates outwards from the source as time progresses and does not flow in concentrically, (4) quantum theoretical: the changes of state in the measurement pro-cess of a quantum system are irreversible, and (5) cosmological: the universe is expanding.

In what sense does psychoanalysis deal with interactions that are time-reversible? In a way, psychoanalytic treatment claims to provide a /limited/ means of time travel. We aim to bring the past into the present, the here and now – not just to explore it but to work it through, thereby revis-ing it before sending it 'back'. Furthermore, by doing this, we propose that we can change the course of the future, if by this we mean emanci-pate the analysand to be less overdetermined by the 'past' in his future choices. However, we know full well that this 'past', supposedly stored in memory, has *not* been frozen in time; it is *not* an ancient artefact saved from history, stored and kept safe from decomposition. The past may have been repressed, but the repressed is alive and in constant flux. Thus, what reappears in the transference is not the historical truth but psychic reality enacted in external. And as we know, by the end of his life, Freud was quite pessimistic regarding the potential of psychoanalysis preventing any future symptoms or suffering.[10]

As for the second law of thermodynamics, many have previously lik-ened the idea of the always-increasing state of entropy in the universe to the Freudian idea of the death drive. Others have vehemently argued against such an analogy. But whether we compare Thanatos to entropy or not, as individuals, we do face this as an existential reality. The ego is, first and foremost, a bodily ego – and the body cannot escape ageing. For the human subject, one thing is certain. Time is not reversible. We can progress and we can regress, but we can never escape the lived reality of time – the unavoidable truths of the depressive position.[11] The reality prin-ciple will defeat the pleasure principle. Libido will flicker away. We age, we lose abilities, energy, and aspect after aspect of life – and we die. For the analyst and the analysand, the finitude of life is, after all, our shared experience of time.

Notes

1 In clinical psychology, studied as our capacity for focused attention, and in contemporary treatment paradigms, colonized through so-called mindfulness practices.
2 It is this gap that manifests time.
3 *The Shadow of the Object: Psychoanalysis of the Unthought Known*, Christopher Bollas, 1987.
4 *Fear of Breakdown*, D.W. Winnicott, 1974.
5 *Transference: The Total Situation.* IJPA, Betty Joseph, 1985.
6 Remembering, repeating, and working through, *SE* XIV, Sigmund Freud, 1914.
7 All of this pertains only to neurosis, of course. If something destroys our capacity for repression, the mind is fragmented. If we lose the ability to forget, i.e. transform 'events' from conscious to unconscious, we drown in an endless present, where events consciously are happening all at once – as in posttraumatic stress disorder.
8 If the time shown by the analyst's clock should differ from that shown on the analysand's clock, we could, of course – not entirely jokingly – talk about the relativity of analytic time. Only, in psychoanalysis, the asymmetry of the situation dictates that the time of the first clock is the correct one, and debate over this will merit interpretation.
9 *Our Adult World and Its Roots in Infancy*, Melanie Klein 1959.
10 An outline of psychoanalysis. *SE* XXIII, Sigmund Freud, 1940.
11 The equilibrium between the paranoid-schizoid and the depressive positions. In: *Clinical Lectures on Klein and Bion*, John Steiner, 1989.

References

Bollas, C. (1987). *The Shadow of the Object: Psychoanalysis of the Unthought Known.* London: Routledge
Freud, S. (1914). Remembering, repeating and working through. *SE* XIV
Freud, S. (1940). An outline of psychoanalysis. *SE* XXIII
Joseph, B. (1985). Transference: The total situation. *International Journal of Psychoanalysis* 66, 447–454
Klein, M. (1959/1975) 12. Our adult world and its roots in infancy (1959). *Envy and Gratitude and Other Works 1946–1963* 104, 247–263
Steiner, J. (1989). The equilibrium between the paranoid-schizoid and the depressive positions. In: Anderson, R. (ed), *Clinical Lectures on Klein and Bion.* London: Routledge
Winnicott, D. W. (1974). Fear of breakdown. *International Review of Psychoanalysis* 1, 103–107

Chapter 7

Encounters with Chronos

François Hartog

The encounters that follow are my own, but since each amounts to meeting, emphasizing, or translating the temper of our times, this turns out to be something beyond one person's intellectual itinerary. My thoughts on time were inspired, reworked, and spurred on by such encounters.

Let me start with two names, two notable watchers of time. First, Michel de Certeau (2016), who declared that "three centuries of objectifying the past" had rendered time "a taxonomic tool the discipline applies constantly yet unthinkingly" (p. 90). As surprising as that statement was when I read it, by now, it has become a truism. Modern historiography, with all its positivism, fixation on chronology, stockpiling of facts, its frenzied aversion to anachronism, was acutely diagnosed by Certeau, yet Jules Michelet, my second name, had already offered a suitable reply in his journal entry of 2 September 1850: "May I be the link between times!" (1962, p. 126). Have we here a megalomaniac? Perhaps. Is he applying a taxonomic tool? Certainly not!

Did I start out as a watcher of the present? Not at all; my first efforts took me in the opposite direction. Partly, 1968 had burst our illusions. And I had opted for faraway times (ancient history, extending even to Homer) and places (during a year spent traveling around the world). So I embarked for the Indian Ocean, the Malay archipelago, and the South Sea islands. I packed Joseph Conrad and Victor Segalen, but in my bag, I also had Claude Lévi-Strauss's *Tristes tropiques* and some blank notebooks. A word in vogue was "alterity," which I certainly sought, as I did different temporalities.

Some years passed, and an encounter with the writings of the anthropologist Marshall Sahlins started me toward what I soon dubbed the regime of historicity. What Sahlins (1985) showed was not only the immersion of

DOI: 10.4324/9781003660118-7

those "islands in history" but their generation of a distinctive, unique form of history that he called "heroic" (p. 34–54). Here, we find a *real* history of kings and battles, for the simple reason that the history is made by none other than the king. No caesura divides present and past, and no attention is paid to what modern Western historiography calls events, namely those things that occur only once. In this temporal regime, characterized by the reabsorption of the past by the present, events never occur; they only recur, inasmuch as all are "identical with their original" (1985, 58). To overcome the structure–event opposition that had waylaid so many, Sahlins proposed going beyond a single historical concept to consider a range of temporalities.

Hawaii and New Zealand, the sites of Sahlins's investigations, offered materials for substantiating and extending Claude Lévi-Strauss's division of societies into "cold" and "hot" types. That much-discussed and -debated distinction, which was soon famous, amounted to a model, insisted Lévi-Strauss, its heuristic value something like that of Rousseau's state of nature. Close to the "zero of historical temperature," the former type appears to be driven by the "dominant concern to persevere in their existence"; the latter draws on "greater differentials between the internal temperatures of the system" for "change and energy." In conclusion, such "hot" groups "interiorize history . . . and turn it into the motive power of their development."[1]

In Sahlins and Lévi-Strauss – one a partisan of an updated structuralism, the other the very father of structuralism, so far as the French were concerned – I found a real sensitivity to clashing temporalities and the discrepancies of historicity. This was in the 1960s, when many historians – not just the Marxists – and intellectuals cast structuralism as an enemy of history, an "antihistorism." Lévi-Strauss's "view from afar" had (already) enabled him – unlike the evolutionists, the Marxists, and Sartre, who hoped that all would make themselves "a man in, by, and for history" – to "provincialize" the history of Europe, casting into a relativized perspective the modern concept of history and its claim to universality.[2]

Structuralism – the term soon encompassed a broad range of practices – emerged during a postwar period marked by a resistance to confronting the recent past. The years 1939 to 1945 were off-limits. Instead, one was urged either to "face into the wind," as Lucien Febvre put it in 1946, or to give up events and embrace long durations, as Fernand Braudel proposed. An analogous movement swept philosophy, where it was out with the subject and in with structures or systems, whether the topic was language, the unconscious, or the "death of man" – at least, of man as found in the humanities.

Assembling a special issue on structuralism in 1967 that inevitably profiled Lévi-Strauss, Lacan, Althusser, and Foucault drove the editor of *Esprit* to wonder, "How can they lay claim to progressivism and the need to change the order of things, while rejecting history, which Lévi-Strauss in particular sees as nothing but an epiphenomenon of ethnography?" The position is contradictory. He concluded, "In the end, this amounts to rejecting not only human agency, *praxis*, but the very possibility of the event."[3]

The regimes of historicity

Reading the historian Reinhart Koselleck was, under the circumstances, illuminating. In *Futures Past*, he set out to frame a theory of historical time centered on the concept of experience (*Erfahrung*). For alongside the times of nature, astronomy, geology, and God, there is space for a truly historical time. Since the latter half of the eighteenth century, "history no longer occurs in, but through, time. Time becomes a dynamic and historical force in its own right."[4] Such a time, conveyed by progress and conceived as an acceleration, functioned as actor and agent in the minds of those who witnessed the French Revolution.

Two metacategories preside over Koselleck's theory of historical time: experience and expectation. Their very generality enabled him to apply them, throughout his work, to setting the conditions for all of history. And as they crisscross both past and future, the categories are well suited to "thematizing" historical time. He made them the two poles – the "space of experience" and the "horizon of expectation" – between which historical time takes shape. The perpetual acceleration of modern time has forced ever wider the gap between experience and expectation, threatening a rupture. By evaluating the modern world through the growing experience–expectation gap, one might explain its major crises.

Odysseus and historicity

Much as I believed Koselleck's to be the most promising route, it became clear that I needed to pin down my ideas about "historicity." The solution, for me, could be found long before the nineteenth century and the deliberations of German philosophy. In that scene from the *Odyssey* that brings

Odysseus and the Phaeacian bard face to face, we have, I feel, one of the earliest encounters with historicity. It plays out in a way that is emblematic, possibly primitive, certainly revelatory. Odysseus asks the bard to sing for him the story of the wooden horse, meaning the sack of Troy and his own triumph. So precisely does the bard relate the details of that event – as though he had seen it in person, the hero admiringly notes – that Odysseus weeps.[5] A yawning gap abruptly opens, as the destitute fellow listening to the song, who has lost everything, right down to his own name, confronts the wily warrior of a decade earlier – himself. Impossible for Odysseus to reach across the distance separating him from the glorious hero of old, who had been likened to Achilleus, greatest of the Achaians. That sudden awareness of an unbridgeable divide between two selfs is what I call "historicity." There are words and categories that Odysseus needs to rise to the occasion, but they do not belong to him – yet. Grasping the past as such, in its "pastness," as a past that is at the same time his past, all that eludes him, and he is unable to say, "That was I, and this is I."

But he hears the bard sing the praises of a certain Odysseus and manages to face and overcome that final challenge. When the "he" of the song is spoken as though he himself were dead and gone, the hero takes possession of his name, declaring, "I am Odysseus." From that moment of "recognition," the poem sets out to unite the man he once was and the man he has become. Here, we have, I believe, the birth of historicity. Before the modern era, before the philosophical implications of *Geschichtlichkeit* were set out, one's relations to the past had taken a form that we may legitimately call today "regimes of historicity" – the *Odyssey* proves this.

The French Revolution: a case study

Before proceeding further, allow me a few words about the concept of the regime of historicity.[6] I insist on "historicity" rather than "temporality" to emphasize the precedence given to how time is experienced. As to "regime," it seems to me better than "form" or "type" because of its flexibility, its dynamic balance, for one speaks of a dietary regime, a political regime, a regime of winds, an engine's regime, and so on. In each case, an assortment or mixture or assemblage of constituent elements is combined according to shifting proportions. Much the same can be said of the regime of historicity: it assesses the temporal categories of past, present, and future specific to an era, a place, a social category, so as to crown one of the three as the leader.

Consider as a rich case study a time of intense temporal disorientation: the French Revolution. Careening into one another with concussive force are two regimes, what the revolutionaries call the "*ancien régime*" and something new, a regime in the making up to (at least) the king's death. On one side stands the old regime of historicity, prizing above all the past as experienced by the king, the Church, and the nobility. This corresponds to the *ancien régime*, whose members soon take to prefacing their titles with "former." On the other side, urged ever onward, paces that new regime ready to break violently with a "hated" past, to erase its every trace. They fancy themselves moderns, devotees of reason and the Enlightenment. They face forward, into the oncoming future, wishing only it would hurry. Robespierre called for an "acceleration" of the Revolution.

From 1789 to 1815 or 1830 extends an in-between, with the *ancien régime* abutting the early date and the modern regime the later. Those decades unroll after one regime of historicity and before the next. The past – even a recast past – reigned over the former, a dynastic order. The future reigned over the latter, and all were expected to make great haste in its direction. Those seeking evidence that time had sped up found it in the rapid rise and fall of political regimes, which sowed further confusion over the era. Such battles over temporality, the old and new societies going at it during the Restoration, provided Honoré de Balzac with the backdrop to his *Human Comedy*.

Chateaubriand and Tocqueville

His life and, even more, his literary decisions render François-René de Chateaubriand the representative of that in-between. In 1789, he was twenty years old, and his life changed forever. One of the losers in the Revolution, until 1830, he remained true to the Bourbon cause. Yet his first book, published in 1797, made clear his view of the new order of time as irreversible. Quite a few of his contemporaries lacked that insight. The breakthrough of 1789 left a rent in time, an unbridgeable strife between the old regime of historicity and the new, borne on modern time.

"I found myself between two centuries, as though at the confluence of two rivers," he wrote as he approached the conclusion to his memoirs, "and I plunged into the troubled waters, regretfully leaving behind the old shore on which I was born, my hopeful strokes taking me toward an unknown shore."[7] Speaking "from his coffin," Chateaubriand piles up dates, telescopes them, returns to the same places from later moments, and brings who he is face to face with who he was. Slipping back and forth between past and present, over and over, he is no Odysseus. By visiting himself, he becomes his own memory place (*lieu de mémoire*). By assembling past, present, even future, he jumbles the order of time.

The classic articulation of the modern regime of historicity was written by Alexis de Tocqueville, born in 1805 of a family that, like Chateaubriand's, had come out on the losing side of the Revolution. "When the past no longer casts light upon the future, our minds advance in darkness."[8] With these few words, near the end of *Democracy in America* (1840), he acknowledges the conclusion of the old regime of historicity, which functioned so long as light shone from the past, while offering a definition of the modern regime. If mishaps and anachronism are to be avoided, it is up to the future to illuminate the past and the present. Tocqueville viewed France, and Europe more generally, from the future – he had just seen the young United States – which allowed him to make out the unstoppably rising tide of equality, the direction in which history was tending, its shifting meaning. While the past had once drawn on its catalog of lessons to offer guidance, the old regime of historicity had now been inverted: the future was now the telos. An ending to be longed for or feared, something to be worked for or stoically awaited, whether decked in the brilliant hues of utopia or the muted tones of dystopia.

Berlin

One last step remained to be taken. If conclusive, it would justify the entire inquiry. Well then, what of the regime of historicity and the present? Can it help unravel temporal experiences as they occur? To get a hold on this turn to the present, a place and an occasion were needed.

A city between times

It was 1993, a few years after the wall had fallen, and I had traveled to Berlin to do some research. Parts of the wall could still be seen, the city center was nothing but work sites, and the worn facades of East Berlin's largest buildings, scarred by machine-gun fire, attested to a time that had not vanished. And yet already, a debate raged over the proposed reconstruction of the Royal Palace, which had been demolished in 1950. In time, it was rebuilt, but first, the Palace of the Republic had to be razed, as it had become a painful reminder of the species of architectural modernism practiced by the German Democratic Republic – plus it was full of asbestos. Construction of the perfectly restored Hohenzollern palace was completed in 2020, and it stands in the space vacated by the Palace of the Republic. The decisions made in historical, architectural, and urbanistic precincts to bring that about all belong to a politics of temporality.

A city between times – so Berlin struck me as I wandered here and there. Whether from one street to the next or on a single block, here was a temporal patchwork shifting as one moved from one neighborhood to another. It seemed, as I crossed its gaping spaces, its wastes and "shadows," its gashes and scars, that the city had lost its way in time. At the center of the no-man's-land that separated East from West in the time of the wall lay the remaining fragments of the old chancellery and the bunker; this was still a temporal borderland. More starkly, more achingly than in any other place, here, time's unthought burst through. By the light of the regime of historicity's instrument, here, one made out various shapes, a jumble of overlapping forms linked with the city's changing relations to time. The latter dated from Frederick the Great all the way to the wall's collapse, not forgetting the Third Reich and its theory of the "value of ruins" (*Ruinenwert*).

When I returned to Berlin in 2014, preparations were underway for the twenty-fifth anniversary of the wall's fall. Since its construction in 1961, the times of East and West had been out of step, desynchronization the order of the day. One might say that at the time, East Berliners and West Berliners were and were not contemporaries. With its gaze locked on the future, the communist regime of historicity declared itself all-round champion of the "radiant future." To get there, it was full speed ahead – never mind that the horizon was in full retreat. After all, if a classless society was to be born with all haste and hurrah, the self-sacrifice of the present was mandated by history. In the jargon of the day, that was the "impassable horizon."[9]

On 9 November 1989, the wall opened. So began the demolition of that symbol of "communist violence." As with the Bastille in July 1789, it needed to go. Some clever folks bagged up bits of the wall – labeling them *"Original Berlin Mauer"* – and sold them to tourists.

Whereas 1789 marked the inception of a new time – the modern regime – no such reorientation to the future followed the fall of the Soviet Union. No matter how doggedly the commissars trotted out the official forecast of a final victory of socialism over the West, that futurist fairy tale had long been discarded by East Germans. And then there was the pair of experiments the West had initiated in the 1970s, elevating the role of memory while closing off access to the future. As a wave, memory swept across Europe, and people spoke soon of a "crisis of the future." It no longer functioned to drive events forward, and it offered, many believed, dangers. The old belief that children would enjoy a higher standard of living than their parents petered out. All that remained was the present, which would soon extend its reach to everything. So the shift from futurism to present-ism was nearly complete: while East and West followed different paths, both were heading for the present. The former longed for the present it deserved and rejected its sacrifice in the name of a perpetually deferred future. The latter had already embraced presentism, where the present declared itself its own horizon in spite of assigning memory a preeminent role. Between the two places separated by the *no-man's-land*, the present functions as an intersection, a common denominator, though the textures and the presuppositions of the two presents differ. On one side, the present has finally arrived, while on the other, there is only the present.

So much so that once the excitement surrounding "unification" had sub-sided, the rush to pull down the wall and restitch, refashion the urban fab-ric and in so doing erase all trace of the wall yielded to – did this surprise anyone? – efforts to preserve it or restore sections. It would be allowed neither to fall to ruins nor to vanish from the urban landscape. But could it be erased without forgetting it? The solution lay in turning it into a memory place, a concept already drawn up and available. As to the brief, it com-prised a commemorative duty, lives to be honored, a lesson to be taught, and a message to be conveyed to the young. This was realized in 1998 with the creation of the vast Berlin Wall Memorial. Sixty meters of wall, just as it stood before the fall, constitute the memorial's central element. Shutting off the space are two six-meter-tall steel plates standing at right angles to the wall. An incision through space, bringing time to a halt, this iron curtain is quite literal. Visitors survey the wall from a balcony much like a watchtower, as they would have seen it from the West when the German Democratic Republic still existed. Brought to perfection, the art of museumifying reifies the vision of the victor. As the brutal sign of futur-ism's failure in the East, those fragments of the wall have passed wholly into presentism, where memory dwells and commemorations set the tune.

Memory and memorials

Berlin had revealed to me, in a specific place, in motion, the coexistence of temporalities that intersect, conflict, and tangle, and the city also convinced me that the regime of historicity could expose and explain the shifts in how time was experienced in Germany over more than a century. Hidden in the no-man's-land that has since been erased, buried with the last traces of the führer's bunker is time's unthought, as Berlin invites, encourages, forces us to acknowledge. Conceiving and directing the politics of extermination took place here. By denying the very humanity of certain human beings, that politics rendered impossible all faith in human progress. The futurism that lay at the core of the modern regime of historicity, fueled by the idea of progress, had been grievously wounded.

A full realization of this truth did not dawn on Western countries for decades. But I am quite certain that in that moment, any sense of a future sustained a formative, permanent wound, condemning it to the unthought. Not for a long time did I understand that my birth in 1946 (shortly before the conclusion of the Nuremberg trials) rendered me, like many others, the child of a gray zone pervaded by silence and a time that never advanced. *Angel of History*, Anselm Kiefer's sculpture of 1989, also bears the title *Poppy and Memory*, words that pay homage to Paul Celan. The work depicts a time that has not budged since 1945, a paralyzed history. As an allegory of the angel of history, Kiefer offers, nailed to the ground, a massive bomber that has completed its fatal flight. Time has also come to a halt for Jacques Austerlitz, the character whose last name provides the title of W. G. Sebald's novel published in 2001. For Austerlitz, time came to a stop in 1939, when the last Red Cross convoys left Prague's railway station full of refugee children.[10]

The great change in our relations to time precipitated reactions, most notably the inauguration of what Pierre Nora called the "memory years." *Shoah*, the film Claude Lanzmann completed in 1985, is the most striking and poignant product of that era. To make a film of memory and about memory, he drew from his interviews shot in the present – and from them alone – what he called the "immemorial." As Lanzmann explained, "The inhuman event, which occurred in my lifetime, was thrust back due to its very inhumanity . . . into a nearly legendary *in illo tempore* [lit., "at that time," i.e., before recorded history], as if outside of human time." His film set out to launch time, which had come to a standstill, back into motion.

Those decades witnessed a flourishing of memorials, museums devoted to memory, and memory places, and states joined in, unfurling politics of memory.

Restored to its status as a capital, Berlin assumes an emblematic part in this era. And there, the role assigned to memory and memorials is certainly important. Fairly late came the Memorial to the Murdered Jews of Europe, which opened in 2005. Not far from the bunker, set in no-man's-land, the memorial comprises a field of scattered steles made of gray concrete, something like a ruined cemetery. Might the goal have been to unearth the unthought, to rule out all forgetting? Here, after all, is the spot where the politics meant to eliminate the Jews was dreamt up in hopes of erasing every trace of them. But this cemetery cannot be a cemetery: those remembered here left nothing but smoke, and no one has collected their ashes, and no cemetery has their ashes. As a memory place – the willing visitor can be utterly absorbed by the place – the memorial wishes to turn all of the missing into the dead. It offers them a symbolic burial, so that even here, time will manage to begin again, so that the living, the survivors, may find their footing once again in time. It acts as a temporal instrument, evoking the past within the present of those – each of those – who visit.

A new epoch in time: the Anthropocene

Had I wished to, I might have stopped there and declared success in my journey through the regime of historicity. The watcher of time I had gradually become could have announced the job complete. After all, I had written a book about the regime of historicity, employing a dynamic relation between three concepts derived from Christian time: *chronos*, *kairos*, and *krisis*. In my ending, I had come back to the present. Others could pick up where I had left off if they wanted to.

One problem: time never stops. Another encounter convinced me to stay the course a bit longer, as once again, change swept across the temporal landscape, provoking mounting confusion. It was in 2017 that I took the opportunity of a visit to the University of Chicago to initiate a conversation – which has continued ever since – with the Bengali historian Dipesh Chakrabarty. Among the very first to think deeply about climate change, he applied his experience as a historian of globalization to the task, and a series of exchanges with scientists made possible his great book, *The Climate of History in a Planetary Age* (2021).[11]

Entering a planetary age

A time new to us has burst the bubble of presentism. Yet this is a quite ordinary sort of time, only extremely protracted, known far and wide – studied closely, broadcast widely – by its manifestation in global warming. Humanity has entered a new era, quickly labeled the *Anthropocene*. A sequel to the Holocene, the label applies to a new geological era. Why "Anthropocene"? The name conveys that humanity itself, the human species, has attained a geological force that can be measured. Presentism had long grown accustomed to seeing nothing beyond itself; suddenly, the vastness of future and past loomed, the Earth's billions of years. The planet's past stretches back 4 billion years, while the future presents a different immensity, the threat of a sixth mass extinction within a few centuries. As hard as it is to conceive, we have crossed the threshold. Already, the climatologists tell us, the changes we have made to the climate will persist for 100,000 years. Nothing we do today can fix that.

From the instant a limit is set, a qualitative change is imposed on the period leading up to that end point, since it becomes a time of the end. Just such a limit has recently entered the picture, as we confront the possibility of an end, not of the Earth's time but of the world's. Christians previously conceived of a new time opening through the *kairos* of the incarnation; the time of the end had begun. But none save God could determine when the final day would fall. Under such circumstances, it is not surprising that our time resounds with the jeremiads of attention-hungry apocalyptists from various denominations, catastrophists, collapsologists frantic and mild, and other prophets of doom. Given the nature of the presentist regime – its impatient dismissal of duration, its rejection of history and the possibility of progress, its susceptibility to the emotions of the moment, its inability to formulate any philosophy of time – all of those expressions of confusion and angst have a generous (and highly rated) platform.

But others have, thank goodness, responded differently to this new state of things, which calls for considering the world and the planet as a pair. Let us consider only the issue of time: here, we must figure out how to hold together the world's temporalities in all of their multiplicity, conflicts, and contradictions, along with the temporalities of the Earth system. Might it be useful to consider an anthropocenic regime of historicity to suit the advent of a new climatic regime and what Chakrabarty calls a "planetary age"? Until now, it was hard enough to keep track of the world's many different temporalities, with their tendency to multiply, split, and (even) individuate. (Connected watches imply an extreme situation, where every person dwells in a unique temporal bubble.) From now on, all of those temporalities will have to be considered, in a lump, along with those of the Earth system, though the two are essentially incommensurable. They must be held together, though a problem of scale makes any true correspondence impossible. And all this at a time when presentism, that quintessential regime of unthought time, seems likely to extend its run for many more seasons.

Rethinking futures of the past and the present

"We cannot continue to believe in the old future if we want to have a future at all."[12] Bruno Latour is quite right, particularly since "the old future" belonged to the modern regime of historicity. Through that future, thanks to that future, Western states managed to impose their preeminence and their domination on the world. But presentism wrecked the future. Addicted as it is to acceleration, presentism means perpetual emergencies ever more pressing, one catastrophe leading to another. The solution offered is ever more powerful, ever more rapid computers; data and the lightning progress of AI will save us. We are assured that our daily needs and the economy can both be managed via just-in-time inventory: out with bothersome stock, in with the click.

The state of emergency has recently extended to the climate, as cities and nations have acknowledged. A resolution declaring a climate emergency for Europe and the world was adopted by the European Parliament in November 2019. When the presentist regime issues such an announcement, it makes a state of climate emergency the most visible mode of inscription in both the public space and the political calendar. Here is an emergency all right, but the climate emergency cannot be resolved by a few clicks. Something must be done, but capitalism cannot be hauled down in a day, no matter how convinced we are of its culpability, and there is no single one-size-fits-all solution for all 8 billion human inhabitants of the Earth. In the long series of emergencies to which the world's communities are subject, where shall we place this new crisis? Some of these must be existential threats, more urgent than others. For instance, how about the emergencies those communities face due to the COVID-19 crisis? How are those emergencies to be prioritized? Who will do it? Once again, we have run up against challenge posed by the future – or rather, by the futures, whether short term, long term, or very long term. We should take them all into consideration, keeping them separate and distinct without overlooking their interdependence and (partial) overlaps. But the very nature of emergencies, with their crushing demands, makes this impossible. Then, once an emergency has spread everywhere, time will be tied into a knot, triggering a massive jumble. At that point, it will cease to be time's unthought; it will become the time we do not know how to think, unthinkable.

The past, which had been absorbed by the presentist bubble, is now reappearing. Its most noticeable trait, just like the future's, is a change in scale. If the past extends to billions of years – life began 3.5 billion years ago – the middle no longer belongs to human beings. Roughly 300,000 years old, *Homo sapiens* was born yesterday, basically. Any claim to exceptionalism has to be reevaluated once that perspectival shift "naturalizes" the human species. Human beings are animals, after all, though not necessarily exactly the same as the other animals.

This perspectival shift also has consequences for what historians have designated and carved off as the "historical" past. Now that the end no longer looks like a Heaven belonging to the elect and no longer belongs to a fully realized humanity, and rather than an endless cycle of similar cycles, it has assumed the form of an ongoing, looming extinction, it is high time we returned to the past, pinpointing missed opportunities, poor decisions at the crossroads, and blocked possibilities so as to draft another history. What used to be a positive teleology must be reverse engineered to serve as a negative teleology: "Here is what we should never have done!" Why? Because it led us to the new era where we now stand, one step at a time. Reader, it is up to you to draw lessons from all this for today, before it really is too late. No matter what, whether we validate or reject the past, it did occur, and the result is the structure of Western time. As with the futures, we should hold together the various pasts without setting them in conflict with one another or by accommodating them all neatly to one another by ignoring differences in scale.

Finally, the impact of the Anthropocene on presentism has destabilized its framing of the present. As a daunting future swings up onto the horizon, it is no longer acceptable to exist pent up in a present that sees nothing but itself there. We are seeing a revival of the paired scissor blades: the time of the end and the end of time. By the latter, I do not mean the end of the time of the Earth but rather that of the world's *chronos* time, something that human beings made and controlled. Conclusion: presentism, in all of its blindness, is no longer tenable, must be tolerated no longer. And yet it persists. No matter how many criticisms, rejections, and shocks it has suffered, presentism is not in decline. It exists and has expanded: a digital world is an innately presentist world. Here is the contradiction. At a moment when we must come wholly to terms with our futures, there is a significant fraction of the world's population whose ways of being, living, and thinking are daily becoming more and more presentist. While there are many causes, there is also a mental block. On the level of the presentist *mentalité* or *habitus*, what matters is the instant, the reaction, the emotion, "my" (always editable) choices. The news is saturated with it. The social networks thrive on it.

Here, one last time, is Tocqueville, on his return from America. "When the past no longer casts light upon the future, our minds advance in darkness." He wrote that in 1840. With those words, he enshrined the end of the old regime of historicity and accorded the modern regime an epigraph by inversion: when the future casts light on the past (and the present), our minds no longer advance in darkness. France's past becomes legible, and now, the Revolution can be inserted, its role and position now certain, in the history being written. But when history continues further, our minds will once again advance in darkness should the light of the future flicker or go out. This arrangement, I believe, made possible the presentism that appeared first in the Western world. Only those bits of the past and the future that serve to justify it are illuminated by this self-sufficient regime, this autonomous present, which claims to produce its own light. The media age provided the initial momentum. Nowadays, the present sits in judgment on the past while fretting about a future it deems unpredictable, threatening, or both at once.

But over the course of a few years, the situation has altered. With the advent of the planetary age, light is once again shining from the future. Our minds should no longer advance in darkness – but the light is black. Under the modern regime of historicity, a structure now revived, the future occupied the leading position and illumined both present and past. But this new regime differs from the modern, which we had fashioned in its entirety. Yes, humanity has become a geological force, which accounts for our partial involvement, and yet it seems best to flee the future now heading our way, or at worst, to slow it down a bit. Here are the twin mottoes of the hour: Renew your belief in the future! A future the very opposite of the radiant one! The future is, now, a hardship for a human race raised on a diet of futurism for nearly two hundred years, only to be seized by presentism fifty years ago.

It once seemed sufficient to take into consideration the past and the future. That is no longer true. We now think in terms of pasts and futures, their implications various, different, yet connected. Sorting out the tangled skein is no easy task. Still, it might be possible if the present regained all of the youthful vitality it possessed as *kairos*, a possibility if shortsighted presentism were rejected. When Charles Péguy commented on Henri Bergson, he highlighted the "place of presence of the present."[13] A moment of decision, the present allows us to reflect on time. How very different is presentism: its longing to annihilate time renders it literally unthinkable.

The most recent test: COVID-19

January 2020 gave us the COVID-19 epidemic, which swiftly became a pandemic. Unforeseen though not unforeseeable, it triggered a crisis that brought the entire world to a halt, upending familiar temporalities. I still have not completed my modest journey: what about COVID, time, and the regime of historicity?

To grasp the virus, one must consider it as a total and global social fact. After all, it opened the way to unique temporalities. Consider, first, the temporality of the virus itself, initially a mystery to medical science. When the decision was made to quarantine the population so as to slow transmission – in France, that happened in March 2020 – an unprecedented time was created. A ruling in favor of life and against the economy suspended the ordinary time that flows according to pocket planners. From that moment on, days have ticked past while the present does not budge. One by one, each of the temporalities woven into our daily lives has been affected. As synchronization fails, we fall under the temporal sway of a capricious dictator: our viral master. Again and again, politics tries to seize control by establishing a horizon, but the wily virus always breaks free and resets all of the clocks. *Chronos* time has no appeal for this unpredictable strategist.

Driven to extremes by the pandemic, presentism loses any sense of direction. The state of emergency never lets up, has no limit; think of the health emergency that is announced then extended endlessly. Never before have societies endured such dictatorial emergencies. And where emergencies multiply, so do delays (lag times). They are inseparable. The sole possible response to all the emergencies and delays is ever-accelerating acceleration. Recourse to the image of the footrace has grown tiresome. Every policy decision initiates one more leg in the race against the virus. Can we win this time? Will we? Are we losing? Have we already lost? For two long years, a lexicon provides the twenty-four-hour news outlets and the op-ed pages their bread and butter: emergency, delay, acceleration, planning (more accurately, its negation). Government hears, more than any other criticism, about its failure to plan ahead. Criticism – accusation – incrimination: the jump from one to the next happens so easily. But wait! Don't we live in a just-in-time world? Don't we tally up hospital expenses with a view to reducing all of those costs? In our presentist world, what has planning become?

The lockdowns that yielded novel temporalities may have reinforced presentism, but they also generated real doubts. Days never varied, yet somehow, each brought new worries, new classroom regulations, new takes on all that seemed so settled the day before. Suspending time did not render the hours any the less painful. And there were those who opted never to return to the time of before. Those with the means abandoned the big cities, adopted new rhythms for work and life – they left behind the presentist cage. At the same time, the COVID-19 crisis made our daily lives and the economy even more digital than ever, tightening the grip of presentism.

And we carried out a search for precedent, scrutinizing once more those earlier epidemics. That useful revival of *chronos* time did not go far enough, because we needed to push much further back to address the question of evolution. Placed in that framework, COVID appears as nothing but a brief episode. Let us adjust the scale one last time. Compared to microorganisms that trace their lineages back 3 billion years, *Homo sapiens* is a Johnny-come-lately. So to understand COVID-19 – a concrete case – we must weigh different pasts with their different durations and their various significances. This grave crisis offers us an opening, a chance to wake up, and our recovery should be a time to redouble efforts to reform our relation to time. All creatures, microbial and human, belong to the history of biology: they were here before us and may well outlast us.

Several recent epidemics have been caused by coronaviruses; COVID-19, the most recent coronaviral disease to leave its mark, is a zoonosis, its precise origins unknown. Zoonotic diseases are on the upswing due to the quickening pace and scale with which wild ecosystems are being destroyed. Since the 1950s, the Earth has witnessed a Great Acceleration, and this destruction is a part of that exponential increase in every aspect of human activity. Add to our futures, with their distinctive temporalities, an epidemic future and all that it implies. Made of surprise and fear, a *kairos* time tends to emerge from viral outbreaks; this crisis may be mildly severe or very severe, triggering a disturbance in *chronos* time or even its suspension. It lasts until the virus adjusts itself to normal time, becoming, as is now predicted for COVID-19, a "seasonal flu." A virus has a cycle that can be grasped, bothered, slowed, even perhaps accelerated to exhaust its mutability, but nothing can be done to halt or destroy it. Life after the virus is a life with the virus.

That epidemic future, lest it carry on as an unthought temporality, must be added to the list of futures we mean to hold together and weigh carefully, since it is a horizon for the entire world. Our temporal shortsightedness ensured that the pandemic would catch us unawares, and yet it has turned out to be congruent with the new epoch we have entered. It feels quite natural for a planetary regime of historicity that hopes to pinpoint the traits of our inchoate historical condition to take account of this epidemic future. A new cosmology stands less in need of a universal chronology than it does a cosmochronology. We shall see.

Notes

1 Lévi-Strauss, C. (1976). The scope of anthropology. In: Layton, M. (trans), *Structural Anthropology* (Vol. II). New York: Basic Books, 29 ("cold" and "hot; "zero of historical temperature"; "change and energy"), 28 ("dominant concern"); Charbonnier, G. (1969). *Conversations with Claude Lévi-Strauss* (Weightman, J. & Weightman, D., trans). London: Jonathan Cape, 33 ("greater differentials"; "interiorize history").

2 Sartre, J. P. (1988). What is literature? In: Ungar, S. (ed), *"What is Literature?" and Other Essays*. Cambridge, MA: Harvard University Press, 183.

3 Domenach, M. (1967, May). Le système et la personne. *Esprit* 360(5), 771–780.

4 Koselleck, R. (1985). 'Neuzeit': Remarks on the semantics of the modern concepts of movement. In: Tribe, K. (trans) *Futures Past: On the Semantics of Historical Time*. Cambridge, MA: MIT Press, 246; Lattimore, R. (trans). (1967). *Homer: The Odyssey of Homer*. New York: HarperCollins, 133–134.

5 Lattimore, R. (trans). (1967). *Homer: The Odyssey of Homer*. New York: HarperCollins

6 Hartog, F. (2015). *Regimes of Historicity, Presentism and Experiences of Time* (Brown, S., trans). Columbia University Press.
7 Chateaubriand, F. R. (1951). Mémoires d'outre-tombe. In: Levaillant, M. & Moulinier, G. (eds), *Bibliothèque de la Pléiade* (Vol. 2). Paris: Gallimard, 936.
8 Tocqueville, A. de (2003). *Democracy in America and Two Essays on America* (Bevan, G. E., trans). London: Penguin, 819.
9 [TN: The phrase belongs to Jean-Paul Sartre, who applied it to Marxism in *Critique of Dialectical Reason.*]
10 W. G. Sebald was born in 1944 in Wertach. Anselm Kiefer was born in 1945 in Donaueschingen. *Au sujet de "Shoah," le film de Claude Lanzmann.* Paris: Belin, 1990, 10.
11 Chakrabarty, D. (2021). *The Climate of History in a Planetary Age.* Chicago: University of Chicago Press.
12 Latour, B. (2017). *Facing Gaia: Eight Lectures on the New Climatic Regime* (Porter, C., trans). Cambridge: Polity, 245.
13 Péguy, C. (2019). Conjoined note on Descartes and the Cartesian philosophy. In: *Notes on Bergson and Descartes: Philosophy, Christianity, and Modernity in Contestation* (Ward, B. K., trans). Eugene, OR: Cascade Books, 184.

References

Certeau, M. de (2016). *Histoire et psychanalyse entre science et fiction* (3rd ed.). Paris: Gallimard

Chakrabarty, D. (2021). *The Climate of History in a Planetary Age.* Chicago: University of Chicago Press

Charbonnier, G. (1969). *Conversations with Claude Lévi-Strauss* (Weightman, J. & Weightman, D., trans). London: Jonathan Cape

Chateaubriand, F. R., Levaillant, M. & Moulinier, G. (1966). *Mémoires d'outre-tombe* (Vol. 1). Paris: Gallimard

Domenach, M. (1967). Le système et la personne. *Esprit* 360(5), 771–780

Hartog, F. (2015). *Regimes of Historicity, Presentism and Experiences of Time* (Brown, S., trans). Columbia University Press

Koselleck, R. (1985). 'Neuzeit': Remarks on the semantics of the modern concepts of movement. In: Tribe, K. (trans) *Futures Past: On the Semantics of Historical Time.* Cambridge, MA: MIT Press

Latour, B. (2017). *Facing Gaia: Eight Lectures on the New Climatic Regime* (Porter, C., trans). Cambridge: Polity

Lattimore, R. (trans). (1967). *Homer: The Odyssey of Homer.* New York: HarperCollins

Lévi-Strauss, C. (1976). *Structural Anthropology* (Vol. II). New York: Basic Books

Michelet, J. (1962). *Journal* (Vol. 2, Viallaneix, P., ed). Paris: Gallimard

Moulinier, G. & Levaillant, M. (1951). *Bibliothèque de la Pléiade.* Paris: Gallimard

Péguy, C. (2019). Conjoined note on Descartes and the Cartesian philosophy. In: *Notes on Bergson and Descartes: Philosophy, Christianity, and Modernity in Contestation* (Ward, B. K., trans). Eugene, OR: Cascade Books

Sahlins, M. (1985). Other times, other customs: The anthropology of history. In: *Islands in History*. Chicago: University of Chicago Press

Sartre, J. P. (1988). What is literature? In: *"What is Literature?" and Other Essays* (Ungar, S., ed). Cambridge, MA: Harvard University Press

Tocqueville, A. de (1835/2003). *Democracy in America and Two Essays on America* (Bevan, G. E., trans). London: Penguin

Chapter 8

Discussion of François Hartog's paper
Encounters with Chronos

Joëlle Picard

Comment on François Hartog's "Chronos"

How does one become a "watcher of the present"? This is how François Hartog defined himself in the lecture he gave us at the Symposium on Time. Indeed, what is the path taken by this member of what he himself called "Vernant's gang", a true heir of that school, that is to say, by making it his own and by distancing himself from it?

My commentary will be that of an analyst; I have no legitimacy to discuss the content of the conference, but I can speak of what reading and listening to François Hartog has awakened in me in terms of reflections, not only on my own clinic but also on the relationship between his intellectual approach and ours. And if Time is not a psychoanalytical notion, the question of time is constantly underlying our practice.

Two main axes appeared to me. The first one is related to the organisation of this Symposium: the confrontation with other scientific fields can highlight a relationship in the thought process and thus enlighten our own. And this even if it is a field as distant from ours as the theory of relativity.

The second axis is more related to the content of François Hartog's works and his conceptions of historicity. We can think that the various cultures favour or inhibit the expression of unconscious elements that potentially exist in every human being. And other human sciences linked to sociology (certain types of ethnology or history in particular) highlight, through myths, stories, valued, or prohibited behaviours, what can be found in a particular subject; they can enlighten us by highlighting what will not appear to us at once, because we share it with our patient.

From his first book, "Le Miroir d'Hérodote",[1] François Hartog situates himself "on the side", and what he says about his project, concerning the

DOI: 10.4324/9781003660118-8

Scythians described by Herodotus, defines his position as very different from what would be a "classical" historian's position, looking for the elements of a precise knowledge on the Scythians, that of a mythologist looking for the origin of myths surviving among peoples who would be their heirs. But, he says, he will focus on "Herodotus' Scythians", that is to say on what Herodotus writes about them and which manifests an unexpressed conception of the otherness of these "barbarians", a conception in this case not specific to the author (about whom we know little), but to the Greeks of the fifth century to which he belongs. Treat a text as we treat the manifest content of a dream? Of course, with other references and from another perspective; but should I underline another kinship with our approach (the questions are more important to us than the answers): this first book ends with . . . questions[2]! Which will lead to further research.

Although I was not aware of it when I read this first book, it was probably the author's position, close to the one I was beginning to have as an analyst, even more than the content of the book, that made me continue to read the following ones.

The interest in ethnography, which is already sensitive to it, will go through the reading of Sahlins and will make it possible to approach the shores of Time, time as we live it in spite of ourselves in the historical period and the place where we live, first in "Les Régimes d'Historicité",[3] a major book, and moreover widely recognised as such and abundantly translated, then, more recently, with "Chronos",[4] an in-depth study of "Christian time".

In "Regimes of historicity", François Hartog demonstrates the variation in the conception and perception of time in our Western culture. An ancient, cyclical, but endless time is followed by a Christian time, beginning with the birth of Christ, enlightened by his coming and tending towards a predictable but indeterminate end, and a modern time, heading towards a radiant future thanks to progress, before the present era plunges us into a totalitarian present, without past or future (and memory is not history). This general presentism is quite noticeable in our daily life as analysts, who see more and more patients (misnamed) asking for a quick, almost immediate solution to their difficulties; and it is under this term that the request is made, the suffering is not named as such.

Without following François Hartog's presentation step by step, I am going to share with you the thoughts that this text has inspired in me, in the associative way that is our daily life.

In Berlin's "places of memory", we are confronted with the power of the non-verbal: from Libeskind's architecture in the Jewish Museum to the silent steles of the memorial to the murdered Jews, there is no room for words, which would fail to express the unthinkable (and the project is very different from that of Yad Vashem, where the names of the murdered are inscribed). Survivors often kept silent about what they had experienced, some committed suicide, many went through pathological episodes close to what was called at the time "manic-depressive psychosis", and most said nothing for years, trying to live. On an individual level, for some of our patients, there are areas of unthinkability, of psychic emptiness, where only traces remain. And like what François Hartog says about humanity after the Shoah, for them, there is no future, no past, only events and the present.

We build ourselves with the unconscious elements that, at a very early age, are transmitted to us, not only the mother's personal unconscious but also her cultural unconscious. In the beautiful words of Piera Aulagnier: "At the moment when the mouth meets the breast, it meets and swallows a first sip of the world".[5] In writing this, I am referring to the idea that different cultures would favour or forbid certain expressions of the unconscious (Devereux).[6] And the historical variations in the experience of time, the regimes of historicity, are cultural, non-conscious variations. Can we make a link between transgenerational traumas, evoked by the historian, individual traumas that are familiar to us, and a certain number of clinical situations? For some years now, we have been increasingly confronted with what Scarfone has called the "unpassed",[7] i.e. elements, generally traumatic, that have not been psychically integrated; they remain both present and unperceived. We can think that not only personal traumas are involved but that these patients grew up after the Shoah and the nuclear bomb, bathed in presentism, with, transmitted "ethnically", this zone without psychic representation, reflecting an unthinkable present and above all outside the individual history. The role of the analyst will then be to encourage their representation, and this will take the form of past events, i.e. the patient will be able to construct a history for himself instead of keeping within him an obscure and present memory. Clio and not only Mnemosyne. In writing this, I am referring to François Hartog's distinction between Memory and History and the current cult of heritage, presentification, and petrification of elements of the past, in relation to the interest in History.

Can we also make a link between cultural presentism and the "permanence of the object" at an individual level? For a certain number of patients, qualified as "borderline" or "narcissistic personalities", one of the questions that emerges clinically is that of the "permanence of the object": we are faced with subjects for whom the relationship exists only in the presence, the link to the other (whether by telephone or virtual technology). There is an impossibility of evoking the absent, of keeping a representation of it, and a decisive step in their analytical treatment is, for them, the possibility of continuing their sessions between them, of continuing to represent the analyst – or the analysis – during interruptions, holidays, or more simply between two sessions. Doesn't the situation of presentism that we are experiencing favour this way of living the relationship to the other, whereas other modes of historicity would perhaps help these subjects to find a greater continuity of being?

This also reminds me of the passage in *The Odyssey* where Ulysses weeps and does not recognise himself when he hears the story of the capture of Troy, where his ruse (the wooden horse) was decisive. When we read: "Ulysses has neither the words nor the categories that would allow him to master the situation, that is to say to apprehend the past as such (in its *pastness*), as of the past and as his past", could we not replace Ulysses with some of our patients? In particular, a patient who, during her childhood and adolescence, cried when she saw her baby toys, usually put away at the back of a cupboard. For a long time, this remained mysterious to her, but then, she became aware that for her, this baby was another. Like Ulysses, she did not recognise herself. Ulysses, in a way, found himself when he was able to recognise himself in his name, his identity; should I say that one of the major difficulties of my patient was to recognise herself as having her own identity, a temporal continuity too. We have known for many years that part of the work of analysis, for a certain number of patients, allows them to give a historical form to their fantasies, conflicts . . .., even though this "family novel", constantly repeated, is only a representation of their inner life. I don't want to make an amalgam between historical and/or ethnological thinking, concerned with what may be common to a group, and psychoanalytical thinking, but we can consider that elements may appear in a subject which, in other cultures, are commonly found. And Ulysses, here, is a character from *The Odyssey*, and moreover a mythical character, that is to say the creation of a human group, at a given time and place, transmitted by an :author", Homer. As such, this episode of *The Odyssey*, in addition to the appearance of a historicity, as François Hartog points out, bears witness to a society where the name gives an identity, that is to say the recognition of oneself as a subject, here by the social environment, individually by the first other. And Ulysses will have allowed me to be more sensitive to what this patient could say about her relationship to time by hearing it also as the reflection of a fragmented Self.

More generally, what relationship does psychoanalysis have with time? It was born in "modern times", and Freud, from this point of view, was very much of his time, driven by the idea of progress: for him, psychoanalysis was a science, moving towards discoveries that would shed light on the origins of neuroses and enable them to be resolved. At least at the beginning of his work, before events such as the war (1914/1918) shook this optimism . . . and probably his conception of a "modern" regime of historicity.

Moreover, the question of time is central for an analyst and opens up many paradoxes: the time of each session is fixed, subject to the clock, as are the days and hours of the sessions, but the duration of a treatment is indeterminate. During the session, time is no longer the same, what has been experienced becomes present, is (re)experienced in the moment; hence probably the idea that the unconscious does not know time. On this point, I can only quote from the very beginning of François Hartog's talk: *the event does not happen, it returns, insofar as it is perceived as structurally "identical to the original event"*. Is this the history lived in the Pacific Islands or the transferential reliving on our couches? Would analysts therefore live, in their practice, under different regimes of historicity simultaneously: the linear time of the clock, the cyclical time of the return to the present of past experiences, and a modern time stretched towards the future of the end of the analysis?

And in our still very presentist era, how can we take the time for analysis? Moreover, if imminence of a climatic catastrophe experienced by some people puts the future into perspective, does this make the long process of psychoanalysis, which requires at least medium-term confidence in the future, futile?

There are many other comments to be made, but our readers will certainly enjoy this stimulating text, which bears witness to both a personal journey and a thought anchored in its time.

Notes

1 d'Hérodote, L. M. (1980). *Essai sur la représentation de l'autre*. Paris: Gallimard.
   The Mirror of Herodotus: The Representation of the Other in the Writing of History. University of California Press, 1988.
2 "What is a historical text? What constitutes it as such, by what means can it be recognised? What (particular) effect does it have?"
3 Régimes d'historicité, Présentisme et Expériences du temps" (expanded edition, Seuil, 2012).
   Hartog, F. (2015). *Regimes of Historicity: Presentism and Experiences of Time*. New York: Columbia University Press.
4 Chronos, L'Occident aux prises avec le temps" (Gallimard, 2020).
   Hartog, F. (2022). *Chronos: The West Confronts Time*. Columbia University Press.
5 Aulagnier, P. (1975). *La violence de l'interprétation*. Paris: PUF, 43.
6 Devereux, G. (1983). *Essais d'Ethnopsychiatrie Générale*. Paris: Gallimard, Tel and Devereux, G. (1972). *Ethnopsychanalyse Complémentariste*. Paris: Flammarion.
7 Scarfone, D. (2014). L'impassé, actualité de l'inconscient. *Revue française de psychanalyse* 78(5), 1357–1428.

References

Aulagnier, P. (1975). *La violence de l'interprétation. Du pictogramme à l'énoncé*. Paris: PUF

Devereux, G. (1972). *Ethnopsychanalyse Complémentariste*. Paris: Flammarion

Devereux, G. (1983). *Essais d'Ethnopsychiatrie Générale*. Paris: Gallimard

Hartog, F. (1988). *The Mirror of Herodotus: The Representation of the Other in the Writing of History*. University of California Press

Hartog, F. (2015). *Regimes of Historicity: Presentism and Experiences of Time*. New York: Columbia University Press

Hartog, F. (2022). *Chronos: The West Confronts Time*. Columbia University Press

Scarfone, D. (2014). L'impassé, actualité de l'inconscient. *Revue française de psychanalyse* 78(5)

Chapter 9

Kairos and Chronos. Clinical-psychoanalytical reflections on time

Bernd Nissen

Freud writes: "The processes of the system Ucs are timeless; i.e. they are not ordered temporally, are not altered by the passage of time; they have no reference to time at all. Reference to time is bound up, once again, with the work of the system Cs" (Freud, 1915e, p. 187). The timelessness of the unconscious is here defined by Freud *ex negativo*, in relation to a vectoral, chronological concept of time as it exists in the Cs system.[1]

At the same time, "cathectic innervations" (Freud, 1925a, p. 231; see also 1900, 1920, 1925b) are sent from the unconscious into the Pcpt-Cs system in periodic bursts and matched with the perceptions of the sense organs. Freud, to my knowledge, does not examine the interplay of inner sensations and outer perception. But the pleasure in the increase of stimulation cannot be thought of purely quantitatively but is likely to be related to a qualitative feature (see Freud, 1924, p. 372). Freud suggests that rhythm may be this factor. Thus, quality appears to be a decisive factor in the development of the concept of time (see Freud, 1920, pp. 4, 31).

According to Freud (1900), psychic qualities can be grasped by consciousness. This raises the question of the relationship between Ucs and (Pcpt-)Cs for temporal processes. Freud did not explicitly consider this relationship, but Green (2002) and Reed (2016) have examined the relationships between conscious and unconscious in relation to temporality[2] and illustrated them with the example of "Emma", among others (Freud, 1895, p. 447ff (SE 1:356ff)). As a child of eight, Emma was "indecently" touched by a grinning shopkeeper. Despite this incident, she goes alone into the store one more time, "as though to provoke the assault", but never after that. She has an "oppressive bad conscience" (Freud, 1895, p. 445). The incident is repressed. As a pubescent girl, she sees two shop assistants laughing as she enters a store and leaves in "shock" (p. 445). One of

DOI: 10.4324/9781003660118-9

the two would have "pleased her sexually". I do not want to go into the psychic dynamics here (see Freud, Green, Reed) of how the early scene is unconsciously connected to the pubertal one and leads to a release of affect. I would like to emphasize just this one aspect: the unconscious, here the repressed, is timeless but pushes into the Pcs/Cs via associative connections and leads to symptom formation. For an *observer*, the shock affect is made up of two events, the past and the present. In Emma's psyche, however, the childish scene is unconsciously present in the shock affect, or more precisely, it is there as actual.[3] I.e. the unconscious complex, which is timeless, pushes into a present experience, thereby creating an event which is partly torn out of the chronological time event: it becomes embarrassing-actual.

Breakdown

In his reflections on breakdown, Winnicott developed *en passant* a very interesting theory of time. The breakdown has happened, but there was no 'ego' that could have experienced it. The breakdown is a rupture in going on being, whose rupture points cannot connect afterwards. Silent, empty, symptomless – in contrast to other nameless states: around autistic and autistoid states, defenses develop such as second skin formations, autistic objects; hypochondriacal states operate with false signifiers, e.g. fear of cancer; psychosomatic states express the nameless on a somatic level, etc.

Breakdown hardly shows itself during treatment, even to a trained observer. Silent, empty moments may flit by. But they begin to condense. Suspicions, perhaps unease, germinate. A difference arises: the analyst suspects that he will be confronted with 'something' unknown, an unknown that is different from unconscious material. The analysand suspects that 'there' is still 'something' 'somewhere', in my experience often located in the body.

This is what Winnicott describes:

It must be asked here: why does the patient go on being worried by this that belongs to the past? The answer must be that the original experience of primitive agony cannot get into the past tense unless the ego can first gather it into its own present time experience . . .

In other words, the patient must go on looking for the past detail which is not yet experienced. This search takes the form of a looking for this detail in the future.

(1974, p. 105)

Later, he says:

The patient needs to 'remember' this but it is not possible to remember something that has not yet happened, and this thing of the past has not happened yet because the patient was not there for it to happen to. The only way to 'remember' in this case is for the patient to experience this past thing for the first time in the present, that is to say, in the transference. This past and future thing then becomes a matter of the here and now, and becomes experienced by the patient for the first time.

(1974, p. 105)

Winnicott also makes it clear that the breakdown is not a trauma (p. 106) and that the breakdown "is carried round hidden away in the unconscious" (p. 104). But this unconscious has nothing to do with the known forms of the unconscious.

In short, the analytic pair senses that something uncanny, intangible, threatening is approaching from the future, showing up in the present, eventually becoming past and hopefully, in part, unconscious.

Time in a simple model

A theoretical model (see Nissen, 2021, 2023, 2025 for details) in the tradition of Freud and Bion might look like this:

There is a pre-conception of the relationship between mother and child that is pushing to its realization. The pre-conception makes use of raw sensual, non-psychised elements in order to be addressed. At the moment of realization – that is, the real encounter between mother and child – the child is there, the mother is there, and the relationship is there. At the same time, the experienced and expected states are there but completely without quality. This moment, which I have described as a presence moment, is neither conscious nor unconscious, without reflexive 'Ego', paradox-circular, qualityless. Here, only a pure perceptual consciousness exists. This moment could contain time and space. It pushes towards sublation into a presentational symbol. I borrow the term "presentational symbol" from Susan Langer (1942). It captures a state that is so complex that it can be preserved only in the presentational symbol, never fully described discursively.

What the moment of presence will have been is determined *nachträglich* in the presentational symbol. But this determination follows its own laws: first, the relationship is *established*. Then we *discover* asymmetrical states, i.e. structures and dynamics, in the analysand. At the same time, however, what is discovered is a *creation* of the analytic pair. What is discovered shows up in the present moment and yet will have been created by the pair. With the sublation into the presentational, the created discovery is then fixed, whereby this fixing is beyond the sovereignty of the participants, a *superimposed subjugation* (see also Ogden, 1994). Nevertheless, it must be empirically true, i.e. connectable. After all, the participants believe that they are empirically sharing the same thing. Presentational symbolism with its fuzziness makes much possible here, but it remains, strictly speaking, a mistaken belief – a reassuring mistaken belief. A psychically qualified conception has emerged, witnessed by the analyst.

Speculatively and heuristically, we can assume in this model that time and space appear in the present moment, and the time dimensions and the place emerge with the presentational symbol: something approached the pair from the future, showed itself in the present, and, having become psychic, can become past. But the simple formula, time gives birth to times, is not true. Because the time dimensions ran ahead as a kind of preparation to the event of time, even if they came into being only through time.

An attempt to understand time[4] clinically

The empirical reality of psychoanalytic practice is, of course, much more complex than simplified models. I will therefore give an example that I have already discussed several times (e.g. Nissen, 2013).

Breakdown and autistoid perversion

The patient was a very intelligent woman, about 40 years old, who had developed, among other things, a perversion: faeces trigger violent sexual excitement, they are eaten, she smears her whole body with faeces and urine. On two occasions, she became seriously infected by these practices, once life-threateningly. The perversion was practised alone, though also with frequently changing other objects, although "the others as persons, as individuals, do not play a role" (patient's words). She frequently allowed herself to be anally penetrated, unprotected, in such states of arousal. At the same time, she suffered from inflammatory bowel complaints that required frequent visits to the toilet and caused diarrhoea.

This perversion became apparent after she met a sex-addicted man, whose sexuality was infused with an extreme death-drive quality.

Because of an infection, so the narrative, she wasn't ever taken into her mother or father's arms in her first year of life. The narrative can be doubted in its absolutely literal form: the mother must have held her child, even against medical advice. It could be felt that the mother loved her, beamed at her, played with her, and laughed.

Today, I am assuming that the patient experienced breakdown conditions that persisted undetected for decades and were awakened by the contact with the sex- and death-addicted man. The patient formed autistoid defences, but the life-threatening infections alerted her to the danger. The autistoid parts in the perversion are not difficult to discover: second skin formations, autistic forms and objects. The autistoid perversion can be understood as a defence against breakdown, but equally as a *nachträgliche* expression of a breakdown, even if this form of representation keeps everything hidden.

But both the breakdown and the autistoid perversion are *psychically* non-existent (see Bion, 1970, p. 9), not even in treatment, whether as shame, disgust, sexual arousal, split-off activity; as suffering, problem, conflict, destruction, hatred, annihilation. Nor did it emerge sensually, for example in its greasy, stinking features. No echo, no emotional resonance arose in me. When she spoke of the practices, it was as if she was communicating that she had completed some routine task. *If* I thought I sensed anything at all, it was a distant, alien, near-death, objectless lostness.

The emergence of the breakdown in treatment

At the same time, the beginning of the analysis was surprisingly lively. The patient very quickly seemed to feel secure and safe in the treatment: when I came to the practice from my office (I have to walk along a small garden path so that patients who come early can see me – this patient always came a few minutes early), she beamed at me. She looked like a toddler who sees the mother and begins excitedly wiggling her hands and kicking her legs. Although there was no such motoric discharge, her eyes were shining and I had a feeling of deep joy inside me. The treatment was a joyful get-together: we had a similar sense of humour, liked the same things – and the patient was well aware of this.

If I interpreted this happiness or even connected it with "not being held", a moment of "nothingness" arose – before she cheerfully continued. Her descriptions of the perversion or her oppressive forlornness remained equally blanked out, e.g. when she told me, without any psychic or objectal connection, how she used to drive aimlessly through the city at night in her car.

I think we can observe in this dynamic the coexistence of a psychically alive world and psychic non-existence, which do not seem to touch each other. From the tension between jubilant happiness and psychic nothingness, microcosmic attunements developed between the patient and myself. Thus, these joyful, excited atmospheres produced a guilt-ridden discomfort in me, caused by the fear of acting with and through this entanglement without addressing the nothingness, the nameless. I found no way to bring it into treatment.

But more important were enactments that immediately began to unfold in the relationship. One day, for example, the patient began to avert her gaze when I arrived. She gave me a little smile, lowered her eyes, or looked away. I was irritated.

More and more, there was an increasing tension in the air which is difficult to describe, an apprehension and fear of a realization which, at last, culminated in a touch. Instead of sitting on the chair and waiting, the patient had gone to the toilet. When greeting me, she hesitated to shake hands. Her hands were still damp. She was silent. She then said she had wondered about shaking my hand as before the session, at home, she had had her faeces in her hands. She had washed her hands thoroughly, also using disinfectant, but felt she had to wash her hands again here. For the first time, I felt a moment of disgust and inner distancing.

This dynamic can be understood as follows: on the one hand, the difference between nameless states expressed in perversion and conceptualised, objectal states gives rise to pre-conceptual container-contained (cc) structures as well as to premonitions of this very nameless. In the stagings, the cc structures are increasingly aligned with the sensed nameless and vice versa, without the participants knowing what is in store for them. They move towards 'something', while at the same time this event, the moment of presence, comes towards them. In this dynamic, an emerging pre-conceptual expectation directed towards the future dominates. This process is flanked by chronological time dimensions as they prevail in consciousness: the scenes constantly sequence and condense.

At the same time, there has to be a glimmer of faith that the cc structures can withstand the force of the breakdown that will occur and that the nameless-destructive can be rendered harmless – even if there can be no guarantee of this.

So there are two things: the expectation that the nameless will show itself in the moment of presence and the hope that the moment will point to a reality that can have a curative effect.

Presence moment

One day, the nameless showed up and the perverse-autistoid contents poured into a session: the patient indicates that she has practised "it" once again for herself alone in the bathtub and uses a projective identification to communicate this. This led to a presence moment in pure perceptual awareness: the scene was there, the patient, myself, and the relationship were there. It is like Schrödinger's cat: in the presence moment, the breakdown is there, but whether it becomes re-traumatizing or can be sublated is not decided. A and -A at the same time, but without any quality. What the moment will be will only be revealed *nachträglich*.

Do time and space reveal themselves here? Gadamer writes: "Time is for being to happen" ("*Zeit ist, dass Sein sich ereignet*" 1969, p. 143). What being the philosopher Gadamer has in mind, I do not know, but here the psychic, which is not sensory, is there in order to become – as Winnicott puts it.

The psychic cannot become if the sublation into the presentational symbol is absent. Without this sublation, the present moment threatens to become traumatic. In the treatment situation, with the return of the Cs system, it was possible to grasp and name the secondary qualities. For I had discovered how the patient felt in the bath scene: lonely and ceasing to be; how the atmosphere is: freezing cold, only the warmth of the excrement is there; how the excrement tastes: inflammatory, even if this is not a taste. I understand that the men with whom she shares the perversion are not objects but represent an agglutinated, extended self. And I am certain that the death will triumph, that the patient will die very soon. She must have felt the dissolution, the nothingness. I don't remember my words, but I told her what the central emotional qualities were and appended to the interpretation: "you are going to die this way." The interpretation was not a masterpiece. But the patient accepted it. Interdependent with the qualifying of her state, the patient perceived an object that is able to contain and is related to her in a concerned way. The presentational symbol is a discovery: the pair discovers the reality of the perversion practised in the bathroom. It is only in the *Nachträglichkeit* that the scene becomes *psychically real*! At the same time, the naming is a creative act of the pair, e.g. "inflammatory taste". And the pair is subject to the power of the sublation. It is not foreseeable e.g. how the words will work, what power they will unfold. For the patient, the postscript had become the most important: "you are going to die this way." This sentence paraphrased her breakdown experience, her psychic dying as an infant. With this sentence, she knew she had a chance to live.

The presentational symbol sublates the moment of presence in the Hegelian sense. In the presentational, the perversion is there; above all, central features of the breakdown are there in all their force: a disintegrating self in an objectless forlornness, held together by a faecal second skin. This facticity has now become *psychically real*. But this state shows itself in a relationship that is containing – and *nachträglich*[5] finds a name and a meaning in the presentational symbol. Thereby, at the same moment, it is no longer there.

In this way, the perversion that was practised in the bathroom can for the first time be discovered as *psychic reality*. Analysand and analyst now know what the patient is doing in the perverse act. The analyst thus also becomes the keeper of reality and a witness.

Time as place

This latter aspect points to an important difference in grasping the presentational, which is also important for understanding time. With the presentational symbol, a conception has come into being. This conception is the realised pre-conception of the expectation of a relationship. It gives the qualified elements the place to accumulate and connect, that is, the previously nameless elements that we paraphrase as dissolution, annihilation, lostness. The related elements stabilize the conception interdependently.

The analyst now has the capacity to transform this conception into a thought. What we call thought here is the conception that survives the absence of the object and thus enables the self to think the presently absent object and the past and future present object.

This has interesting consequences for the understanding of time; for the analyst, past and place came into being with the presentational symbol: the perversion was practised yesterday (past) in the bathroom (place). In it is hidden an early breakdown of the going on being.

In the patient's intrapsychic reference system, things are now completely different: the bathroom scene and the underlying breakdown are present in the presentational sublation. The breakdown is there in the containing relationship and can be experienced in the object relationship without being traumatic. We need to be more precise: in the sublation, the breakdown is there and is – at the same time, named – not there. Both states are present. A divorce between past and present does not succeed. It has to be located differently. Just as a child who has experienced a traumatic fright and in the fright feels held, while the frightening thing is in the room "back there", the patient locates the past spatially "there in the bathroom". The temporal location is thus not in time "past" but in the place where the perversion was practised. The past is the place where it happened.[6]

The realization of the absent object and the times

The conception must, as a consequence, become a thought for the patient. But what does this mean in concrete terms? Let us return to Freud's observation. Sexually perverse impulses push into the Pcpt-Cs, the sense organs provide external perceptions, e.g. faeces. The resulting arousal is channelled into the preconscious systems. But which "memory systems" (Freud) now play a role? If the arousals were merely to connect with the transformed material of the bathroom perversion (the "deed", to use Freud's term), the perverse forces would soon overwrite and erase this discovery and psychic sublation. But the connection happens not with the "pure" discovery of the perversion practised in the bathroom but with the *discovery* of this perversion *in the relationship with the analyst*. If the pure "state discovery" could not oppose the forces of resistance, the knowledge that the analyst knows about the reality, that he cannot be blanked out as an external, separate but still meaningful object (except in a psychotic denial, but that too would be interpretable), is now the decisive catalyst for the transformation of a conception into a thought. With the analyst as the one who has discovered the "deed", the perversion undergoes a breaking that tears it out of the non-psychic performance.

In the absence, the analyst potentially becomes the re-traumatizing object. In the breakdown, the destructive forces were at work. The absence of the analyst connects the patient's psychosomatic system with the absent object of the past. Absence is experienced as a loss of holding; not being held threatens dissolution, unintegration. It is important to understand this dynamic in all its force, not from the perspective of a mature ego. Because in such dynamics, the mature modes of functioning that the patient has undoubtedly developed can hardly be activated. She is at the mercy of an event that is similar to the rupture in going on being. In the patient's experience, the analyst has conjured up the horror of the breakdown – and then leaves her alone after the session. This constellation is the reason suicidal, psychotic, and psychosomatic episodes so often follow in such dynamics with the presentational sublation.

In the transference, it is therefore important to establish oneself not only as an absent object but also as a threatening, re-traumatizing one. Then the states that the patient suffers can be there and interpreted.

These dynamics, being the re-traumatizing object and no longer being it in the interpretations, finally make it possible for the conception to become a thought for the patient. By being the preserver and witness of the reality of a breakdown and by being able to acknowledge his involvement in the suicidal dynamics that follow, the analyst can be recognised as a holding and understanding object. The experience could be paraphrased as follows: "You, analyst, know about my breakdown; you, analyst, leave me alone, expose me to the dissolving fears – but you really understand, so it must be that you are good to me, want me to live." The relationship becomes conceivable even in the absence of the object. Times emerge: the analyst becomes an external object that is absent in the present, was there in the past, and will be there in the future. The actual timelessness of the breakdown, which submerges self and object and is devastatingly threatening, can become a condition that the patient has. Put simply: the patient no longer *is* fear but *has* fear. State and relationship become thinkable, the object becomes relatable.

In the patient, this dynamic took on extreme forms, which I was at the mercy of without a safety net or false bottom. A suicidal pull towards death unfolded in separations: "I don't want to kill myself, but it will happen.

I'm afraid, no, in panic, do you understand, Mr. Nissen? It is killing me, I'm powerless" – panic that the death pull will triumph, that patient and analyst are powerless. We both knew how serious it was. Just as I was uncertain whether she would come to the next session, the patient was uncertain whether I would discontinue the treatment and arrange a psychiatric admission, which is what all my colleagues advised. But this termination would probably have become a real re-traumatization. My realization that I had really become the re-traumatizing object for the patient, watching impassively, could be brought into the session. At that moment, I was the re-traumatizing object, and at the same time, I was not, because with the naming, the identity had become difference. The suicidal horror ("it will happen!") was – fortunately – banished. The establishment of tenses allowed other dynamics to emerge – object use.

Use of the object

This passive-endured dynamic is subsequently transformed into an active-omnipotent one: the object is used. Winnicott writes: "The baby creates the object but the object was there waiting to be created and to become a cathected object" (1969, p. 713). That is, in the focal point of this dynamic, the analyst is there to be created. This creation takes place through the destruction of the object. The object survives the destruction. The destruction and retrieval of the object are omnipotent processes. Paradoxically, the object is destroyed not only because it exists outside omnipotent control but also because the destruction places it outside omnipotent control (see Winnicott, 1969, p. 713). Thus, it becomes possible to conceive dependence and separateness.

This figure of creation and destruction (a fantastic game of Fort-Da) differentiates not only the self–object relationship but also the use of tenses, which are now no longer tied to a place. If this fantasy detaches itself from omnipotence and the object becomes an external one that I need, the object that is now absent was present before and will be there again, not vengeful but understanding. A thought can be thought, and with it, times are there.

Summary

Time conceptions and relation are bound to the Cs system, or more precisely, to the Cs and Pcs systems. Freud emphasizes that "the conscious presentation comprises the presentation of the thing plus the presentation of the word belonging to it" (1915, p. 201). The breakdown occurred when there was no ego to experience it. Therefore, it is represented neither as a conscious nor as an unconscious idea. In our case study, it finds its first *nachträgliche* form in the autistoid perversion, which neither establishes a psychic connection to the breakdown nor is itself psychic. It stages itself, i.e. pre-conceptual forms of time appear in relation to the non-psychicized content. This complex only becomes psychically real through the presence moment, but it has to become in the presentational.

Does time show itself here? At least we can say that the conditions for time and for experiencing time show themselves.

It seems very interesting to me that for the patient, the breakdown and its sublation are experienced as present, whereas the discovered event can only be experienced as place. The past is the place where something happened.

The psychic realization is bound to the object; despite the realization, an autonomous ego does not yet exist for the breakdown. For this, the independence of the object must become psychically conceivable through the process of forming a thought and using the object. Only then can an emerging Ego, rising from the abysses of breakdown, think itself, the object, and the relationship. The conception survives the absence. With this thought, past, present, and future times are also there, able to detach themselves from place.

Experiencing time seems to be coupled to the conscious presentation, which rests in the thing-presentation. The processing of the unconscious, which is timeless, enables the conscious presentation of time – evidence for Bion's view that the systems Cs and Ucs are to be understood binocularly.

Notes

1 In my opinion, the dynamics of *Nachträglichkeit* always include both arrows of time, even though one forward or backward time vector may dominate. I will therefore not distinguish between deferred action and *après coup* in the following but always use the German words *nachträglich/Nachräglichkeit*.
2 Green writes: "The unconscious is unaware of time, but consciousness does not know that the unconscious is unaware of time; it does not even know that the time it has at its disposal is miserably short" (2002, p. 37). He emphasizes that regression, e.g. in the dream or in the symptom, is not primarily to be understood temporally but topically (and formally, I would add; see also the excellent interpretation of Green's theory of time in Reed, 2016).

In contrast, the concept of *Nachträglichkeit* is conceived temporally (see here Hock, 2005, p. 293, who sees the diachronic temporal level suspended in the synchronic one and links *Nachträglichkeit* to the latter). Two vectors of time can be discerned in the case of *Nachträglichkeit* (see Freud, e.g. 1895; 1918, p. 72; 1939; Birksted-Breen, 2003, 2009; Dahl, 2010; Eickhoff, 2005; Faimberg, 2005; Hock, 2003, 2005; Laplanche, 1992; Loch, 1988, 1993; Sodré, 2005). In one, the *Nachträglichkeit* follows the chronological arrow of time. In the other, *Nachträglichkeit* works against the chronological arrow of time. In one, the present is interpreted in light of the past, in the other, the past in light of the present, two time frames with a latency inserted. The dispute between deterministic and constructivist-consensual has long occupied psychoanalysis (e.g. the conflict between Loch, 1988, and Pasche, 1988; see Eickhoff, 2005). I am not an expert on the concept of *Nachträglichkeit*, but two objections seem to me worth considering: in my opinion, the reference system of psychoanalysis, the psychic, is missed in the question about a historical-objective determinacy. Historical, factual data do not belong to the psychic reference system. Furthermore, in the debates around *Nachträglichkeit*, the psychoanalyst is given primacy in interpreting the contexts. I do not share these positions either.

3 In a very different theoretical context, Scarfone (2016) speaks of "actual time". With Noë, he distinguishes "the perception of an inert thing from the perception of an event. For unlike an inert object, an event is necessarily said to occur in time" (2016, p. 393). Scarfone introduced a third category: "the Thing". It "stands at the threshold of perception" (p. 393). Its time "is always now" (p. 394): an actual time. See also Baranger et al., 1988.

4 Even in the psychoanalytical sphere, the literature on time is no longer manageable. Summaries/overviews can be found in Abraham (1976), Birksted-Breen (2003, 2009), various works in Glocer Fiorini, L. and Canestri, J. ed. (2009), Green (2002), Gutwinski-Jeggle (1992, 2005), Hock (2003, 2005), Laplanche (1992), Schmithüsen (2004), Nissen (2014), Reed (2016), Scarfone (2016).

5 We can recognize the two arrows of time here: e.g. *Nachträglichkeit* in the chronological vector – here the manifest perversion is an attempt, distorted beyond recognition, to give the breakdown an expression *nachträglich* – and *Nachträglichkeit* working against the chronological arrow of time: in the presentational symbol, the psychological reality of the bathroom scene and the breakdown are shown *nachträglich*.

6 How this place is to be thought of remains unclear. In the experience of the person concerned, it is not likely to be a Euclidean, three-dimensional space; rather, as Bion (1970, p. 12ff) reflects, a point where it happened. An infinite, dissolving space might rather be suspected in the unrestrained breakdown.

References

Abraham, G. (1976). The sense and concept of time in psychoanalysis. *Int. R Psychoanal.* 3, 461–472

Baranger, M., Baranger, W. & Mom, J. M. (1988). The infantile psychic trauma from us to Freud: Pure trauma, retroactivity and reconstruction. *Int. J. Psychoanal.* 69, 113–128

Bion, W. R. (1970). *Attention and Interpretation.* London: Tavistock Publications (Reprinted London: Karnac Books). Reprinted in Seven Servants (1977)

Birksted-Breen, D. (2003). Time and the après-coup. *Int. J. Psychoanal.* 84, 1501–1515.

Birksted-Breen, D. (2009). Reverberation time, dreaming and the capacity to dream. *Int. J. Psychoanal.* 90, 35–51

Dahl, G. (2010). The two time vectors of Nachträglichkeit in the development of ego organization: Significance of the concept for the symbolization of nameless traumas and anxieties. *Int. J. Psychoanal.* 91, 727–744

Eickhoff, F.W. (2005). Über Nachträglichkeit. Die Modernität eines alten Konzepts. *Jahrb Psychoanal* 51, 139–161

Faimberg, H. (2005). Après-coup. *Int. J. Psychoanal.* 86, 1–6

Freud, S. (1895/1950). Project for a scientific psychology. *SE* 1, 281–391

Freud, S. (1900). The interpretation of dreams. *SE* 4, ix–627

Freud, S. (1915). The unconscious. *SE* 14, 159–215

Freud, S. (1918). From the history of an infantile neurosis (the 'wolf-man'). *SE* 17, 1–124

Freud, S. (1920). Beyond the pleasure principle. *SE* 18, 1–64

Freud, S. (1924). The economic problem of masochism. *SE* 19, 155–170

Freud, S. (1925a). A note upon the 'mystic writing-pad'. *SE* 19, 225–232

Freud, S. (1925b). Negation. *SE* 19, 233–244

Freud, S. (1939). Moses and monotheism: Three essays. *SE* 23, 1–138

Gadamer, H.-G. (1969/1987). Über leere und erfüllte Zeit. In: Mohr, J.C.B. (ed), *Gesammelte Werke Bd. 4. Neuere Philosophie II.* Tübingen: Paul Siebeck Verlag, 137–152

Glocer Fiorini, L. & Canestri, J. (ed). (2009). *The Experience of Time: Psychoanalytic Perspectives.* London: Karnac

Green, A. (2002). *Time in Psychoanalysis, Some Contradictory Aspects* (Weller, A., trans). London: Free Association Books

Gutwinski-Jeggle, J. (1992). Trauma und Zeiterleben. Theoretische Überlegungen. *Jahrb. Psychoanal.* 29.

Gutwinski-Jeggle, J. (2005). Pathologische Phänomene des Zeiterlebens. In den Vorhöfen von Zeiträumen. In: Münch, K. et al. (eds), *Zeit und Raum im psychoanalytischen Denken.* Tagungsband der DPV Frühjahrstagung

Hock, U. (2003). Zeit des Erinnerns. *Psyche* 57, 812–840

Hock, U. (2005). Die Zeitlosigkeit des Unbewussten und die Wiederholung. In: Münch, K. et al. (eds), *Zeit und Raum im psychoanalytischen Denken.* Tagungsband der DPV Frühjahrstagung

Langer, S. K. (1942). *Philosophy in a New Key.* Cambridge, MA; London, England: Harvard University Press

Laplanche, J. (1992/1996). *Die unvollendete kopernikanische Revolution in der Psychoanalyse.* Frankfurt/M.: Fischer

Loch, W. (1988). Rekonstruktionen, Konstruktionen, Interpretationen. Vom 'Selbst-Ich' zum 'Ich-Selbst'. *Jahrb. Psychoanal.* 23, 37–81

Loch, W. (1993). *Deutungs-Kunst. Dekonstruktion und Neuanfang im psychoanalytischen Prozeß.* Tübingen: Edition Diskord

Nissen, B. (2013). On mental elements. Based on the example of an autistoid perversion. *Int. J. Psychoanal.* 94, 239–256

Nissen, B. (2014). Versuch einer psychoanalytischen Theorie der Zeit. Zeitschrift für psychoanalytische Theorie und Praxis. *Jahrgang* XXIX, 279–298

Nissen, B. (2021). What is the psychic, how can it be grasped and understood? *The Scandinavian Psychoanalytic Review.* https://doi.org/10.1080/01062301.2021.1930505

Nissen, B. (2023). From nothing to being? Technical considerations for dealing with unrepresented states. In: Levine, H. & Santamaria, J. (eds), *Autistic Phenomena and Unrepresented States. Explorations in the Emergence of Self.* Phoenix Publishing House

Nissen, B. (2025). Circling the nameless. An attempt at an impossible approach. In: Power, D. (ed), *The Somato-Psychic Realm: Analytic Receptivity and Resonance.* London: Routledge

Ogden, T. H. (1994). *Subjects of Analysis.* London: Karnac

Pasche, F. (1988). . . . Arbeit der Konstruktion oder, wenn man es so lieber hört, der Rekonstruktion . . . . *EPF-Bulletin* 31, 22–36

Reed, G. (2016). Refracted time: André Green on Freud's temporal theory. *Psychoanal. Inq.* 36(5), 398–407

Scarfone, D. (2016). Enactive cognition, the unconscious, and time. *Psychoanal. Inq.* 36(5), 388–397

Schmithüsen, G. (2004). 'Die Zeit steht still in rasender Eile'. Eine psychoanalytische Einzelfallstudie zu frühem Trauma und Zeiterleben. *Psyche* 58, 293–320

Sodré, I. (2005). 'As I was walking down the stair, I saw a concept which wasn't there' or, après-coup: A missing concept? *Int. J. Psychoanal.* 86, 7–10

Winnicott, D. W. (1969). The use of an object. *Int. J. Psychoanal.* 50, 711–716

Winnicott, D. W. (1974). Fear of breakdown. *Int. Rev. Psychoanal.* 1, 103–107

Chapter 10

Discussion of Bernd Nissen's paper

Kairos and Chronos. Clinical-psychoanalytical reflections on time

Jasminka Šuljagić

In his contribution, Bernd Nissen has set out the various strands of thought that are based primarily on the theories of Winnicott and Bion, on the field-theoretical concepts and the concept of the analytic third, as well as on his own work developed over years and presented in his many published papers. The conceptual apparatus used here by Nissen consists of the theoretical assumptions of the "breakdown" and "use of the object" (Winnicott), the idea of "preconception-conception-realisation" (Bion), the concept of *"Nachträglichkeit"*[1] (Freud), as well as: "the presence moment" (moment of presence), "presentational symbol", "psychically qualified conception" (in contrast to psychically non-existent).

These theoretical-clinical ideas, presented in Nissen's other contributions (2013, 2015, 2018, 2021), in understanding of unrepresented states, hypochondriacal and autistic disorders, are now developed in the context of investigating the conditions for time and experiencing time, together with the presentation of a dramatic clinical illustration. The pleasantly surprising use of the term "sublation" (*Aufheben*), from the theory of Hegel, contributes to the complexity of this multilayered text in the sense of pushing into [present experience], pushing to its realization. Interestingly, this concept has a twofold meaning: the main one is "that which drives it forward", but the second meaning is simultaneously a negating one (to clear away, to cause to cease, to put an end to) and a preserving one. In this way, we are approaching the logic of becoming, introduced also by *"Nachträglichkeit"*.

Those dynamics are seemingly mostly accentuated here by the presence of the analyst and in the context of an analytic pair (prototype mother and child) rather than through an intrapsychic position as well. This leads us towards the possible realization of the missing perspective of the drive

DOI: 10.4324/9781003660118-10

theory in understanding time in the reading of this text, but we will return to this later.

The main idea expressed in the text, in a condensed way, could be formulated in these terms: explaining how the psychically non-existent, nameless, emerged in treatment, both of breakdown and autostioid perversion (as a defense and a *Nachträglichkeit* expression of a breakdown) in the relationship with the analyst, in the presence moment and pushing its way to presentational. In this way, the processing of the unconscious, which is timeless, enables the experience of time to be linked with the conscious presentation; time dimensions being there "as a kind of preparation to the event of time", emerge with the presentational symbol.

I will open my discussion from the points which Bernd Nissen used to raise the question about time in Freud's theory: "Freud, to my knowledge, does not examine the interplay of inner sensations and outer perception". The exploration of the interplay of inner sensations and outer perception by Freud could be approached with consideration of a criterion for distinguishing between perception and memory and an indication of reality, starting from "Project" (Freud, 1895), where dissimilarity between the wishful cathexis of a memory and perceptual categories is conceived as the origin of thought. It also appeared in "Negation" (Freud, 1925) as a judgement of whether something which is in the Ego as a presentation can also be rediscovered in perception (reality). It is one of the approaches, a perhaps a lateral, but possible one, by which we come to the theme of transposition and discontinuity. This leads us further to Freud's main ideas about time, mentioned at the very beginning of the paper by Bernd Nissen: "At the same time, 'cathectic innervations' (Freud, 1925a, p. 231; see also 1900, 1920, 1925b) are sent from the unconscious into the Pcpt-Cs. system in periodic bursts and matched with the perceptions of the sense organs". This sentence seems to me to be worthy of elaboration.

Still very early on, in his letter to Fliess of 12 December 1897, when he was interested in the "endopsychic myths", Freud wrote about projection "the dim inner perception of one's own psychic apparatus . . . onto the outside and, characteristically, into the future and the beyond" (1954).

We also found "that anything arising from within (apart from feelings) that seeks to become conscious must try to transform itself into external perceptions: this becomes possible by means of memory-traces" (1923).

There are also Freud's remarks about time in the 1920s: our ideas of time seem wholly derived from perception of the method of working of the system Pcpt-Cs., again concluding with a cautious "but I must limit myself to these hints" (1920), and a slightly elaborated and moving paragraph in 1925, ending with: "this agrees with a notion which I have long had about the method by which the perceptual apparatus of our mind functions, but which I have hitherto kept to myself" (1925).

For our theme of big value, there is a footnote which Marie Bonaparte added to her text about time after its reading at the XV International Congress of Psychoanalysis in Paris during early August 1938 and after a letter from Freud about it, written on the same or the day before his short notions of extension of psyche:

> although so far as time is concerned I hadn't fully informed you of my ideas. Nor anyone else. A certain dislike of my subjective tendency to grant the imagination too free a rein has always held me back. If you still want to know, I will tell you next time you come.
>
> (Freud 1960, referred to by Carignani, 2018).

It was in late autumn of 1938, London, and according to her words, Freud was talking more about what had earlier only been hints.

The main thread about the projection of the functioning of psychic apparatus was drawn by him here: "When consciousness awakens within us we perceive this internal flow and then project it into the outside world" (Bonaparte, 1940). Freud here also revealed his idea based on the psychology of attention.

> According to this, the attention which we bestow on objects is due to rapid but successive cathexes which might be regarded in a sense as quanta issuing from the ego. Our inner perceptual activity would only later make a continuity of it, and it is here that we find, projected into the outside world, the prototype of time.
>
> (Bonaparte, 1940)

This idea about the periodic non-excitability of the perceptual system and the proposal that this discontinuous method of functioning of that system lies at the base of the origin of the concept of time was expressed by Freud several times, as it was mentioned by Bernd Nissen, and it could be connected with the ideas expressed in another text from this symposium, "Neurobiology of time" by Arnaldo Benini (2022).

However, if we return to the question of time in becoming, of the time-lessness of the Unconsciousness, could we follow the ideas by Freud also in this realm, and what the expression of "timelessness of the Unc" means at all, how we can understand it, and connect it with our clini-cal practice, perhaps with the impressive case material of Bernd Nissen as well? Bernd quoted Gadamer's "Time is for being to happen", but proposing the solution of Winnicott for this: the psychic, which is not sensory, is there in order to become. We might recall here the concept of primal repression (*D.*: *Urverdrängung*) introduced by Freud. This con-cept is referred to only a few times in Freud's work and is postulated to retrospectively explain "repression proper", with anticathexis as its only mechanism. Primal repression, the first fixation of a psychic representa-tive to drive, is conceived as a mythical introduction of drive into the psychic, the first presentations of the body to the psyche, the origin of unconscious, and a leap from the somatic. It is also the duality introduced into psychic life by the processes of primal repression, a tension between regressive attraction and the formation-reconstruction of psychic pro-cesses. Paths are bi-directional, and we can only know some of them, in a temporality which is quite beyond what is immediate and linear (Šuljagić, 2018, 2022). It is also the realm of our theme, the link between the timelessness of the Unconscious and the temporality and subjective experience of time, a process of the temporalization of psyche. However, there is something additional: through primal repression we come to the difference of atemporality and the timelessness of the Unconscious. We know that in Freud's work, the unconscious mental processes are time-less (unaffected by time, not ordered temporally; time does not change them). It is the realm of infantile amnesia, primary processes, perceptual identity, hallucinatory realization. Speaking about primal repression, we could say that timelessness is different from atemporality, which has to do more with disappearance, with the traumatic dimension, and with the tendency of all drives towards extinction (introduced by Freud in 1920), to return to the previous state up to the inorganic one. Primal repression allows a transition from atemporality to timelessness of the Unconscious and finally, by transforming the disappearance into the oscillation of dis-continuity, to construct temporality. From this point, it is possible for us to think about the temporality of Pcpt-Cs., with the help of the self-perception of its own processes and the role of masochism as the product of fusion of drives.

Those concepts and their elaboration might help us to consider the clinical material of Bernd's paper from one more perspective. We know that in 1924, Freud introduced the notion of primary masochism as the part of the death drive remaining in the organism (not projected), which is then bounded with libido. Many authors further developed those ideas, connecting the concepts of primary masochism and the acquisition of time, masochism ensures duration and internal continuity (Rosenberg, 2010).

Without going into details here of this inspiring thinking or of the presented case material, I would just indicate one of the possible understandings of this narrative linked with our theme of time: the absence of functioning that would have primal repression as the cornerstone, incompletion of primary masochism, inaccessibility of the pleasant passive position due to early trauma, and unbounded death drive searching for enactments with a man "whose sexuality was infused with an extreme death-drive quality", beyond representability.

The reappearing of these states in the course of analysis, as an opportunity to link destructiveness and as a secondary attempt at healing could be understood as slow and dangerous reconstitution of a masochistic core, with risky exaggerations ("a suicidal pull towards death". . . "panic that the death pull will triumph") where the retraumatizing absence might finally become a capacity of waiting, the possibility of appropriation of pain, ability to withstand and represent displeasure and to endure the process of analysis.

In this short sketch, we can assume that it might have then enabled infantile sexuality to take form as an achievement in the psychic life of this patient. Near the end of this discussion, I would also mention Freud's notion of waiting ("always waiting for something which never came") as a fixed model of infantile sexuality (1938), as well as his late description of its tragic dimension, a "daemonic" force at work through repetition compulsion (1920).

Only psychic work as a response to the demands of drives upon the mind allows the line of atemporality – timelessness – temporality to unfold, a possibility of time re-elaboration and its reversals in many directions. Like the famous time machine, as one analyst called it, our psychoanalytic knowledge and practice make it possible for us not only to traverse different time dimensions with our patients but also to participate in time transformation, from the frozen time of traumatic atemporality to bearing the pain of discontinuity and its transposition, with the recovery of regressive paths and hallucinatory pole; from the forces of repetition and compulsion of destiny to remembering and making history; from a linear successive historical perspective to a biphasic opening towards future, presentations, and figurability.

Note

1 It is not quite clear why the explanation of the case of Emma (Freud, Project, 1895), as well as the relationships between conscious and unconscious in relation to temporality, here is ascribed to Green and Reed and not to Freud himself, who had initially described it in 1895, in connection with the symptoms of Emma, and continued to refer to two stages in psychic work until "An Outline of Psycho-Analysis" in 1938.

References

Benini, A. (2022). Neurobiology of time. *EPF Symposium on Time*. Chapter 3.

Bonaparte, M. (1940). Time and the unconscious. *Int. J. Psycho-Anal*. 21, 427–468

Carignani, P. (2018). "Psyche is extended": From Kant to Freud. *Int. J. Psycho-Anal*. 99(3), 665–689

Freud, S. (1900). The interpretation of dreams. 4, *Standard Edition*, ix–627. London: Hogarth Press

Freud, S. (1920). Beyond the pleasure principle. In: *Standard Edition* (Vol. 18). London: Hogarth Press

Freud, S. (1923). The ego and the id and other works. In: *Standard Edition* (Vol. 19). London: Hogarth Press

Freud, S. (1924). The economic problem of masochism. In: *Standard Edition* (Vol. 21). London: Hogarth Press

Freud, S. (1925a). A note upon the 'mystic writing-pad'. *Standard Edition* 19, 225–232. London: Hogarth Press

Freud, S. (1925b). Negation. In: *Standard Edition* (Vol. 19). London: Hogarth Press

Freud, S. (1938). Findings, ideas, problems. In: *Standard Edition* (Vol. 23). London: Hogarth Press

Freud, S. (1950). Project for a scientific psychology (1950 [1895]). In: *Standard Edition* (Vol. 1). London: Hogarth Press

Freud, S. (1954). *The origins of psychoanalysis: Letters to Wilhelm Fliess 1887–1902: Drafts and notes*. New York: Basic Books, Inc

Nissen, B. (2013). On mental elements. Based on the example of an autistoid perversion. *Int. J. Psycho-Anal*. 94, 239–256

Nissen, B. (2015). Faith (F) and presence moment (O) in analytic processes: An example of a narcissistic disorder. *Int. J. Psycho-Anal*. 96, 1261–1281

Nissen, B. (2018). Hypochondria as an actual neurosis. *Int. J. Psycho-Anal*. 99, 103–124

Nissen, B. (2021). What is the psychic, how can it be grasped and understood? *The Scandinavian Psychoanalytic Review*. https://doi.org/10.1080/01062301. 2021.1930505

Nissen, B. (2023). Kairos and Chronos. Clinical-psychoanalytical reflections on time. *EPF Symposium on Time*. Chapter 9.

Rosenberg, B. (2010). (Erotogenetic) masochism and the pleasure principle. In: *Reading French Psychoanalysis*. London: Karnac

Šuljagić, J. (2018). Primal repression and the origin of mental life. *The EPF Bulletin* 72, 47–52

Šuljagić, J. (2022). La Represión Originaria y el Origen de la Vida Mental. *Revista de Psicoanálisis (APM)* 95, 583–599.

Chapter 11

The complexity of the dialogue between neurosciences and psychoanalysis. EPF Symposium Berlin 2015

"Psychoanalysis in 2025"

Jorge Canestri[†]

The predictions

This symposium carries the title "Psychoanalysis in 2025" and wonders what psychoanalysis will be like then. I have been asked to speak on the subject "The complexity of the dialogue between the neurosciences and psychoanalysis", and I shall try to do so by following a path that is not linear and from which I hope some starting points and arguments for reflection will emerge. I shall not speak about the neurosciences as such inasmuch as I am not qualified to do so, and it would in any case be redundant to try and talk about the enormous progress that this discipline has made in the last ten years and that is already well known.

Hypothesizing what psychoanalysis will be like in ten years' time implies making predictions, that is, trying to guarantee rational bases for the decisions that will follow – unless one is motivated by a purely scientific interest seeing that the prediction, together with the reproducible experiments, is at the root of the scientific method, and rightly so. In both cases – scientific interest or giving a basis to the decisions – the experts on the subject matter warn us about the difficulty of this undertaking. The more open and complex a system – moreover connected to and interacting with other systems – the more inaccurate, brief in time (horizons of predictability) and subject to error does our prediction risk becoming.

It is certainly not by chance that W. Heisenberg, in his memorandum of 1927 on the "relation of uncertainty" writes that "In the formulation of the law of causality – if we know the present exactly, we can calculate the future – it is not the conclusion that is false, but the premise. In principle, we cannot know the present in every determinant element."

DOI: 10.4324/9781003660118-11

If this is true for disciplines that deal with factual data of a mathematical nature, it is easy to deduce that the problem becomes much more relevant when dealing with a discipline such as psychoanalysis. In many cases, it happens that the relationship between prediction and decision is inverted, and it is the latter, driven by the underlying ideologies, that will command the prediction and not the other way around.

However, this must not necessarily discourage our reflections about the possible and/or probable future, although we must take into due account some of the recommendations deriving from the experience of the specialists.

The physicist Angelo Vulpiani[1] describes certain contemporary tendencies, already mentioned in the past by illustrious physicists and mathematicians, that are much more in evidence now that a huge mass of data of every kind has become available. Poincaré, quoted by Vulpiani, stigmatizing the excesses of ingenuous empiricism, said that "Science is built with facts, like a house with bricks, but a collection of facts is no more a science than a pile of bricks is a house." The idea of doing without theories, in front of the strength of the empire of data, can take the upper hand in contemporary research.

Two considerations that can be useful regarding the dialogue between the neurosciences and psychoanalysis are, firstly, not to put too much trust in the mass of data and observations coming from research without an overall theoretic reflection, and, secondly, not to confuse the correlation between the events with the causal relations between them. I shall return to this last point later.

Construction of theories. Some epistemological annotations.

If we adopt a post-empirical epistemological stance, we discard the classical distinction – introduced by Hans Reichenbach and reformulated by Karl Popper – between context or logic of discovery and context or logic of justification (Canestri, 2006, ch 1).[2] Furthermore, we affirm that the meaning of the observative terms is a function of "conceptual patterns" and, with Lakatos, we reject a clear-cut demarcation between the history of a discipline and the discipline itself. Lakatos affirms (1976)[3] that in order to understand a theory, one must understand the problems it originally intended to solve and verify which problems it de facto succeeds in resolving. To understand this, it is necessary to reconstruct the situation in which these problems were originally formulated and the modalities by which they were progressively transformed. We could call this a heuristic course of theory. As we could easily demonstrate, the relation between the history and the discipline is essential in psychoanalysis and in the construction of the Freudian theory.

An epistemologist suggests some preliminary remarks in order to define the meaning of a heuristic course of theory:

a   What Popper calls background knowledge is to be interpreted as the groups of facts used in the construction of a theory: background-knowledge-of-a-theory.
b   We must presuppose a three-way relationship between evidence, theory and heuristic progress: i.e. theory-arrived-at-in-a-certain-way (theory with its heuristic).

The author concludes that "if the way in which the theory was constructed becomes decisive for the evaluation of its scientific merits, then – against Popper's ideas – the empirical support is heuristic-dependent" (Motterlini, 1994, pp. 329–330).[4]

What is the importance of these "epistemological annotations" for our reflections on the dialogue between neurosciences and psychoanalysis?

I shall try to give a partial reply by mentioning two Freudian theoretical constructions. I shall do so very briefly in the time that is at my disposal.

Let us consider the Freudian construction of the concept of affect, the concept of representation and of that of drive. It is a very well-known construction, discussed and analyzed by many different authors, and certainly my description does not claim to be original or even particularly precise in the details.

The concept of affect (*Affekt*) evolves in Freud's writings simultaneously with the progressive complexity of his theoretical construction, but if we look at the basis and at the constituent elements of the concept, we could identify two main foundations of it. The construction is inspired by the dynamics of Herbart's representations and by Fechner-Helmholtz's economic hypotheses. Freud's particular interpretation and use of both the above were the origin of the two essential constituents of his theory on the psychic apparatus: representation (*Vorstellung*) and affect (*Affekt*), together with all the specifications relative to them. The introduction of the concept of drive (*Trieb*), conceived as the engine and final ratio of psychic life, completes the theoretical picture.

Herbart's ideas on the dynamic of representations that could create contraposition and therefore a quantitative dynamic include concepts such as resistance (Widerstand), repression (*Verdrängung*), inhibition (*Hemmung*). The works of Fechner (*Elemente der Psychophysic*, 1860) on the measurement of sensations and of Helmholtz on a physiological psychology and on conservation of energy offered to Freud suggestive ideas about the role played by energy in the psychic life (Canestri, 2012).[5]

It is very evident that Freud, like many other thinkers, uses various types of materials linked, as said before, to background knowledge and that, of necessity, become transformed as they are inserted and adapted to the new theoretic configuration.

We find another construction of great interest in Freud's work on aphasia (*Zur Auffassung der Aphasien. Eine Kritische Studie*. 1891). As we know, in this case, the basic material comes from neurology and, even though as he himself said right from the beginning, he does not contribute with new data and observations to a better understanding of the pathology; his work is universally recognized as a cornerstone for the subsequent study and theorization of the aphasias. But of even greater interest to psychoanalysis is the function that this study in the theory of the psychic apparatus, i.e. its overall heuristic value.

Imaginary models and theoretic models

Continuing in the search for a reply to the initial question on the possibility of dialogue, I should like to introduce another epistemological resource that could help us.

As mentioned, in the construction of his overall theory on the psychic apparatus and its functioning, Freud uses, among others, two theoretic models – one derived from Herbartian psychology and the other from the energetic concepts of Helmholtz.

The definition of the concept of model is not easy, especially because it oscillates between a descriptive notion of scientific activity and a concept of mathematical logic, but also because eliminating the ambiguity of the definition automatically implies adopting specific epistemological conception, neo-positivistic or, alternatively, post-empiricist. In any case, as far as we are concerned, it would be useful to adhere to the view of the famous philosopher of science and Cambridge Emeritus Professor Mary Hesse in her seminal book *Models and Analogies in Science*,[6] according to which the model and the analogy are essential in scientific practice and have a considerable heuristic value.

In the introduction to the Italian edition, Cristina Bicchieri in 1980 emphasizes the difference between a theoretic model and an imaginary model. If we define a theoretic model as "a collection of assumptions about an object (or system) that describe it by attributing to it an "internal" structure so that many of its properties are explained by referring to this "structure", an imaginary model would then be a collection of assumptions on an object (or system) that show us what it could be if it satisfied certain conditions that in fact it does not satisfy. The model is understood here in its meaning of "as if . . .".

What is the importance of the aforementioned distinction? In my view, in the two Freudian theoretic constructions mentioned before, Freud uses imaginary models of great heuristic value, even when the object described does not satisfy the conditions prescribed by the theoretic model. To give an example, the concept of psychic energy does not satisfy the conditions requested by the physical model of Helmholtz. Moreover, Freud was well aware of this since he felt it necessary to invent a series of terms to outline a research methodology suited to his needs: scientific fantasies, scientific myths, inventions, intermediate or auxiliary representations.

Imaginary models feed on the material that is available at the time when they are created, and they can be updated according to new discoveries or new *Weltanschauungen*. I think that this type of knowledge is at the basis of works such as those of Pragier and Faure-Pragier (1990, 2007), Moran (1991), Spruiell (1993), Galatzer-Levy (1995), Quinodoz (1997) and myself (2004), although there are differences in approach, psychoanalytical culture and theoretical material used.

The problem of relevance

These brief reflections should help us to confront the question that often arises when discussing the dialogue between neurosciences and psychoanalysis. That is, the relevance that one discipline has for the other.

How can we measure the relevance of Helmholtz's theories on energy to the Freudian concept of affect, the contribution of Darwin's theory of evolution to the whole of Freudian thought, the somewhat paradoxical usefulness of Lamarck's ideas in the writing of *Übersicht der Übertragungsneurosen*? The list could be much longer.

If, as mentioned, theories are constructed with the material available according to background knowledge, the theorists' choices, as well as being conditioned by the general knowledge at the time they are living, are also personal and subject to a variety of conscious and unconscious motivations. The pertinence and relevance of a theory or a discipline to another cannot be determined and resolved by following a linear pattern of the type: how useful for and pertinent to psychoanalysis are the laboratory studies on memory that study memory at the molecular level (Kandel)?

Someone could answer that knowing that it is not possible to evoke a memory without modifying it at the molecular level goes along with psychoanalytic ideas on memory and its therapeutic action. This is true, but I don't think it is the only or perhaps the most significant level on which an interaction or an intersection between theories appears to be particularly significant.

I have purposely used the word "intersection" rather than "interdisciplinary" – an abused term whose use should be limited to those easily identifiable cases in which two disciplines find themselves in the condition of sharing, without conflict, theories, methodologies, epistemologies, languages. Normally, this gives rise to integrated disciplines, also in the names given to them: biophysics, astrophysics, etc.

Whoever reads the first chapter *"Relations entre la science du langage et les autres sciences"* in Roman Jakobson's book *Essais de linguistique générale* will have a good idea of what I am suggesting. It is a chapter with 300 bibliographic items, in which Jakobson examines with curiosity and enthusiasm a variety of disciplines: from the modern version of psychology of language based on the old German *Sprachpsychologie* to genetics, suggesting an isomorphism between genetic code and language; and to physics and the visit of Niels Bohr to the Massachusetts Institute of Technology during which they both debate the relationship and the differences between physics and linguistics and conclude that the opposition between them is unjust. Bohr's conclusions are very pertinent to our discourse when he emphasizes how the information that physics obtains from the outside world consists simply in one-way "indices", while in their interpretation, he super-imposes on the experience his own code of "symbols", thus performing a "work of imagination".

The originality of a theory can rest in the combination of concepts that are already known and even, apparently, not consistently pertinent or relevant to the pursued objective. The good outcome of the result will depend to a great extent on the creativity of the theorist.

The reforming imagination that Bohr speaks of is central in relation to the previous discourse on relevance.

In conclusion, I believe that the relevance of one discipline to another, whether in a detailed manner (one particular discovery) or more globally, cannot be entrusted to a linear evaluation, whether it is based on the identity of the material taken into consideration (memory at molecular level or psychoanalytic level), on the languages of the respective disciplines, on their methodologies or on their epistemologies. The heuristic value that one discipline can have for another is more comprehensive, global and unpredictable (and here again, prediction comes into the picture: it is very difficult to predict which discipline will take greater precedence over another if we take into account previous observations).

It is evident that the debate about heuristics in the intersection between disciplines moves in the area of the well-known context or logic of discovery of Reichenbach and Popper. But the initial epistemological suggestion included an important statement in the area of the context or the logic of demonstration – a statement that justifies my previous discourse. It said that "We must presuppose a three way relationship between evidence, theory and heuristic progress: i.e. Theory-arrived-at-in-a-certain-way (theory with its heuristic)".

This is clearly the case with Freud. His construction regarding the psychic apparatus is made up of material that at first appears to be irrelevant to a discipline based on subjectivity; however, the heuristic power of the elaborated theory is very high.

I think it is useful to also remember that there are various levels within a discipline at which the derivates from other disciplines can or cannot be used.

Let us take the example of Noam Chomsky and his theory of language as being biological (the I-language). We all know that Chomsky produced, in a logical sequence, the theory of generative grammar, followed by universal grammar and by the "minimalist programme", maintaining in his theoretic development, in contrast with other theories (cognitive and otherwise), the nuclear idea of the biological origin of language conceived as "cerebral organ". In spite of this fact, he said clearly on several occasions that it was incongruent and useless to try to use the molecular level of understanding of the functioning of language if our task was to analyze a discourse. Even pre-supposing the existence and the constant action of the molecular level in the production of language, there was no use in invoking it at non-related levels. The same could be said about the interesting hypotheses of the anthropologist Ian Tattersall on the existence of a gene with symbolic capacity, a human version of FOXP2, correlated to the capacity to articulate a language: a fascinating hypothesis to link to others from neurolinguistics such as, for example, the studies of the neurolinguist Andrea Moro, who studies "impossible" grammars at the neurobiological level with neuro-imaging techniques. He offers reliable proof of the fact that the distinction between possible and impossible languages should not be a cultural fact but is linked to brain structure. This hypothesis could, in the long run, have interesting repercussions on our theories on language learning. In this case, as in others, the diversity of levels of analysis is at stake.

It is more than evident that biology, when dealing with human beings, is always implicit at the basic level in any related discipline. The problem arises of knowing how and whether to invoke it and in which cases and at which levels of explanation. What seems certain to me is that formulating theories that are in obvious contradiction with biology should not be permitted when human beings are involved.

I am persuaded of the relevance of neurosciences for psychoanalysis if, and only if, (strong objective correlation), we take into due account all the previous considerations and what follows: i.e. the "ontological problem".

The ontological question: Is the subjective experience of X identical to its physical essence?

I should now attempt to suggest a reply to the "ontological" question.[7]

A first observation useful for the treatment of the "ontological" question is that we must be extremely cautious with the facile isomorphism of language. "Translation" is necessary between different uses of the (apparently) same language used by the various disciplines in question.

In this sense, I am following the concept of "radical interpretation" of the language philosopher Donald Davidson, according to whom the problem of interpretation is already present between speakers of the same language. Translation takes place between different uses of the same language.[8] This is true both between speakers inasmuch as each interlocutor tries to insert the verbal segments articulated by the other into a pattern compatible with the pattern that, for him, confers meaning to similar segments articulated by himself, as well as between different disciplines where we have to carefully ascertain the actual compatibility between the patterns that use apparently identical words.

Let us take as an example the concept of representation (*Vorstellung*) – this concept is used in philosophy, in psychoanalysis and also in neuroscience. J. P. Changeux says that there is a mathematical representation in neurons – the meaning of representation in this case is undoubtedly different from its use in psychoanalysis and philosophy.

A second observation concerns our difficulty in psychoanalysis in conciliating the nomological character of processes with the singular character of events. This conflict always arises between the absolute singularity of each case – a distinctive trait of psychoanalysis – and the necessity for a generalization, that is a requirement for any discipline wanting to be regulated by laws.

A third is that every interpretation of mental facts requires a global theory of psychism and clarity concerning the heterogeneity of the elements that come into play, specifically. This is definitely valid for psychoanalysis but probably also for the neuroscience.

A fourth observation regards the definition of the "methodological empirical basis". The unity of analysis, from an epistemological point of view, is theory. The empirical data with which we work are data of the methodological empirical basis – i.e. they are data that presuppose the use of material or conceptual instruments that, in turn, derive from a theory. A different theory of the instrument (or the use of a different instrument) has an inevitable effect on the methodological empirical basis, on the method itself and, consequently, on the theory. It is rather evident that different disciplines have different methodological empirical bases that, together with the differences in the similarity or even apparent identity of languages, require special attention.[9]

The ontological question requires an ontological clarification about the character of the elements in play, i.e. physical on one hand and mental on the other, and an epistemological specification.

Regarding the ontological clarification about the character of the elements, there are two possible alternatives that can be specified: dualism and monism. The philosopher Donald Davidson (1980)[10] suggests the following specifications: (a) nomological dualism "that affirms that there are correlating laws" between the physical and mental events (interaction-ism, epiphenomenalism), (b) nomological monism "that affirms that there are correlating laws and that the events correlated are one" (materialism), (c) anomalous dualism, "which combines the ontological dualism with general failure of laws correlating the mental and the physical" (Carte-sianism), and (d) anomalous monism, which "claim[s] that all events are physical, but rejects the thesis . . . that mental phenomena can be given purely physical explanations".

Davidson suggests for our consideration three principles that I will describe briefly.

Principle of Causal Interaction: "it asserts that at least some mental events interact causally with physical events" (and vice versa).

Principle of the Nomological Character of Causality: "where there is causality, there must be a law".

Anomalism of the Mental: "there are no strict laws on the basis of which mental events can be predicted and explained".

Davidson argues that the inconsistency between these three principles – considering all of them to be true – is apparent. Moreover, he says that he accepts the identity between mental and physical events but does not accept the idea "that a pure physical predicate, no matter how complex, has, as a matter of law, the same extension as a mental predicate".

The subsequent step states that "the mental is nomologically irreducible: there may be true general statements relating the mental and the physical, statements that have the logical form of a law; but they are not lawlike".

In everyday practice, even scientific, we use summary generalizations, or, rather, approximate generalizations, inasmuch as we do not know a precise law for explaining them.

But these generalizations are of two different classes: (a) the generaliza-tion can be improved by resorting to the same vocabulary used in the first generalization, a vocabulary that corresponds to the final law and to one's own conceptual domain. This generalization is called homonomic. A fit-ting example is given by physics. (b) The generalization obtained leads us to believe that there is an operating law, but in order to enunciate it, we have to resort to a different vocabulary. This is the heteronomic generaliza-tion. From what has been said here, it is clear that Davidson thinks that the general statements linking the mental and the physical are heteronomic, rough heteronomic generalizations.

If this is true, it is not possible to accept the existence of strict psycho-physical laws, inasmuch as languages and conceptual domains are dissimilar (categorical difference).

If we accept these premises, the third principle mentioned, the principle of the Anomalism of the Mental, is the logical conclusion.

This conclusion emphasizes the identity of the mental and the physic but also the fact that there are no strict laws at all which consent us to predict or to explain the mental phenomena.

Even knowing all the physical processes, it is necessary to have a pure psychological schema to interpret behaviors, affects, wishes, fantasies, etc.

To a mental event m1 corresponds a physical event p1 (bijective correspondence), but there is no isomorphism.

As we know, my discussant, Oliver Turnbull, who I thank for having accepted to comment on these notes, has written a very interesting book together with Mark Solms[11] on the relationship between neurosciences and subjective life. Chapter 2 "Mind and Brain. How do they relate?" confronts the mind–body problem, defined by the authors as a philosophical conundrum. Following David Chalmers, they define the existence of an "easy" and a "hard" problem at stake. The easy problem is related to how to investigate the neural correlates of something. The hard must answer how a particular pattern of physiological events makes us conscious. After having analyzed, like Davidson, various possible answers to the question of the relation between mind and body, they propose a Kantian philosophical position regarding the limits of knowledge.

Solms and Turnbull think that the nature of the relationship between brain and mind is not amenable to scientific proof. The problem of causation, different from that of correlation, that we left on hold at the beginning of this comment, reappears here. In the words of the authors: "it is appropriate to describe certain neuronal processes as causing consciousness only within a particular philosophical framework" (p. 47).

They claim for a "Dual aspect monism" (that is not so far from Davidson's anomalous monism even if from a different point of view). I quote: "we are made of only one type of stuff (monist position) but this stuff is perceived in two different ways (hence dual-aspect monism)"; "in our essence we are neither mental nor physical beings – at least not in the sense that we normally employ these terms" (p. 56); "This distinction between body and mind is therefore an artifact of perception. we can never scape the artificial mind–body dichotomy" (p. 56).

In order to finish this discussion, we must return to the "ontological" question – i.e. whether the entities described by the various disciplines coincide.

From a strictly ontological point of view the answer could be yes, as far as we accept the first Principle of Causal Interaction that affirms the identity between mental and physical phenomena. This is the Ontological Monism, materialism, which was also sustained by Freud.

But from an epistemological point of view, the consideration of the second Principle of the Nomological Character of Causality, insofar as we cannot enunciate strict laws but just rough heteronomic generalizations, we are obliged to admit a descriptive dualism.

Therefore, the general conclusion says that the Principle of the Anomalism of the Mental claims for an ontological monism and an epistemological dualism (descriptive, methodological and conceptual dualism).

I hope that this could be of some help in order to disentangle some of the complexities of the dialogue between the neurosciences and psychoanalysis.

Thank you for your attention.

Notes

1 Vulpiani, A. (2013). Problemi e limiti delle previsioni. *Le Scienze* 538, 36–41.
2 Canestri, J. (2006). *Psychoanalysis: From Practice to Theory*. London: Wiley Blackwell.
3 Lakatos, I. (1976). *Proofs and Refutations. The Logic of Mathematical Discovery*. Cambridge. Cambridge University Press.
4 Motterlini, M. (1994). La metodologia dei programmi di ricerca scientifici: una revisione. In: Giorello, G. (ed), *Introduzione alla filosofia della scienza*. Milano: Bompiani.
5 Canestri, J. (2012). Chapter 10: Emotions in the psychoanalytic theory. In: Fotopoulou, A., Pfaff, D. & Conway, M. (eds), *From the Couch to the Lab. Trends in Psychodynamic Neuroscience*. Oxford: Oxford University Press.
6 Hesse, M. (1966). *Models and Analogies in Science*. Notre Dame, IN: University Notre Dame Press.
7 This section is a re-elaboration of a part of my chapter 10 for From the Couch to the Lab, quoted previously.
8 Davidson, D. (1986). *Inquiries into Truth and Interpretation*. Oxford: Clarendon Press.
9 Canestri, J. (2005). Some reflections on the use and meaning of conflict in contemporary psychoanalysis. *Psychoanalytic Quarterly* LXXIV, n1

10 Davidson, D. (1980). *Essays on Actions and Events. Chapter on: Philosophy of Psychology*. Oxford: Oxford University Press.
11 Solms, M. & Turnbull, O. (2002). *The Brain and the Inner World. An Introduction to the Neuroscience of Subjective Experience*. London and New York: Karnac.

References

Canestri, J. (2004). Le concept de processus analytique et le travail de transformation. *Revue française de psychanalyse* 68, 1495–1541

Canestri, J. (2005). Some reflections on the use and meaning of conflict in contemporary psychoanalysis. *Psychoanalytic Quarterly* LXXIV, n1

Canestri, J. (2006). *Psychoanalysis: From Practice to Theory*. London: Wiley Blackwell

Canestri, J. (2012). Chapter 10: Emotions in the psychoanalytic theory. In: Fotopoulou, A., Pfaff, D. & Conway, M. (eds), *From the Couch to the Lab. Trends in Psychodynamic Neuroscience*. Oxford: Oxford University Press

Davidson, D. (1980). *Essays on Actions and Events. Chapter on: Philosophy of Psychology*. Oxford: Oxford University Press

Davidson, D. (1986). *Inquiries into Truth and Interpretation*. Oxford: Clarendon Press

Galatzer-Levy, R. M. (1995). Psychoanalysis and dynamical systems theory: Prediction and self-similarity. *Journal of the American Psychoanalytic Association* 43, 1085–1113

Hesse, M. (1966). *Models and Analogies in Science*. Notre Dame, IN: University Notre Dame Press

Lakatos, I. (1976). *Proofs and Refutations. The Logic of Mathematical Discovery*. Cambridge: Cambridge University Press

Moran, M. G. (1991). Chaos theory and psychoanalysis. The fluidistic nature of the mind. *International Review of Psychoanalysis* 18, 211–221

Motterlini, M. (1994). La metodologia dei programmi di ricerca scientifici: una revisione. In: Giorello, G. (ed), *Introduzione alla filosofia della scienza*. Milano: Bompiani

Pragier, G. & Faure-Pragier, S. (1990). Psychanalyse et science: nouvelles métaphores. *Revue française de psychanalyse* 54, 1391–1706

Pragier, G. et Faure-Pragier, S. (2007). *Repenser la psychanalyse avec les sciences*, Paris, PUF.

Quinodoz, J.-M. (1997). Transitions in psychic structures in the light of deterministic chaos theory. *International Journal of Psychoanalysis* 78, 699–718

Solms, M. & Turnbull, O. (2002). *The Brain and the Inner World. An Introduction to the Neuroscience of Subjective Experience*. London and New York: Karnac

Spruiell, V. (1993). Deterministic chaos and the sciences of complexity: Psychoanalysis in the midst of a general scientific revolution. *Journal of the American Psychoanalytic Association* 41, 31–44

Vulpiani, A. (2013). Problemi e limiti delle previsioni. *Le Scienze* 538

Chapter 12

Afterthoughts

Leopoldo Bleger, Heribert Blass, and Joëlle Picard

Given the clarity of the texts in this book, both the papers and the responses, we prefer to leave readers to create their own path through the topic of time and shall confine ourselves in this epilogue to highlighting certain difficulties that run through the discussions without aspiring to be exhaustive or getting to the heart of the matter. We also wish to acknowledge the fifth text that has been included in this volume – Canestri's paper, which he actually presented in 2014. We felt it had a place here as it presaged insights and answered questions that arose at the symposium eight years later. We hope the reader will not be deterred by the challenges that accompany its conciseness.

With Kant

"Immanuel Kant laid the foundational concept on which the neurobiological research of the sense of time would then develop" – with such homage, Benini joins Münster in making Kant his first pivot. He goes on to say that for Kant, time is not an empirical concept that derives from experience. Both our representatives of the 'hard' sciences remind us of the Kantian postulates: "Time is a pure form of sensible intuition" (*reine Form der Anschauung*) and "time is a necessary representation that grounds all intuitions." For Kant, time is a priori – a 'founding representation' in the philosophical sense of the term, one with which our thinking functions. We could say we think with 'it'. It's a framework for thought rather than the stuff of thought and is intrinsic to much of modern science.

However, Kantian propositions on time and space clash with a key psychoanalytic hypothesis: the timelessness of the unconscious. Freud arrived

DOI: 10.4324/9781003660118-12

at this conclusion about the clash with Kantian thinking quite late in life, writing in 1920:

> As a result of certain psycho-analytic discoveries, we are to-day in a position to embark on a discussion of the Kantian theorem that time and space are 'necessary forms of thought'. We have learnt that uncon- scious mental processes are in themselves 'timeless'. This means in the first place that they are not ordered temporally, that time does not change them in any way and that the idea of time cannot be applied to them. These are negative characteristics which can only be clearly understood if a comparison is made with conscious mental processes. On the other hand, our abstract idea of time seems to be wholly derived from the method of working of the system Pcpt-Cs. and to correspond to a perception on its own part of that method of working.
>
> (Freud, 1920)

This passage clarifies what Freud means by 'atemporal' – "time does not change them (unconscious mental processes) in any way". It also demon- strates the difficulty of giving a definition that is not negative and under- lines the complexity of the notion of '*zeitlos*'.[1]

The first quotation can be 'completed' by a series of others. Here's the second set from thirteen years later:

> There is nothing in the id that could be compared with negation; and we perceive with surprise an exception to the philosophical theorem that space and time are necessary forms of our mental acts. There is nothing in the id that corresponds to the idea of time; there is no rec- ognition of the passage of time, and – a thing that is most remarkable and awaits consideration in philosophical thought – no alteration in its mental processes is produced by the passage of time.
>
> (Freud, 1920)

He reiterates and states subsequently in the same text: "Again and again I have had the impression that we have made too little theoretical use of this fact, established beyond any doubt, of the unalterability by time of the repressed. This seems to offer an approach to the most profound discover- ies" (Freud, 1933). It is striking that he notes this as the "exception to the philosophical theorem" and says it "awaits consideration in philosophical thought" and asserts that "we have made too little theoretical use of this fact, established beyond any doubt, of the unalterability by time of the repressed." The progression in Freud's thought invites us to open our own thinking too to the radical nature of these proposals.

The third quote from 1939, one of Freud's last remarks, is likely to trouble our ideas even more: "Space may be the projection of the extension of the psychical apparatus. No other derivation is probable. Instead of Kant's a priori determinants of our psychical apparatus, I would propose the following: the psyche is extended; knows nothing about it" (Freud, 1939).[2] While initially referring explicitly only to space, he quickly goes on to use the term 'Kant's determinants' – he is speaking not only of suspending Kantian time and space for the id, but indeed of replacing them with the projection of an extended psychic apparatus.

How are we to interpret this hypothesis? The thought we'd like to put forward is this: the permanence of the notion of psychic apparatus.

Biology and the illusion of simultaneity

At the time of Helmholtz, the electrical stimulation of a motor nerve and the contraction of the muscle in response were believed to occur simultaneously based on the principle of a vital force, of *Lebenskraft*. Against this paradigm, the movement around Helmholtz and du Bois-Reymond therefore was, among other things, a rising up "against vitalism". Benini expresses the contemporary understanding very well – the subjective feeling of simultaneity is an illusion, a trick played by the brain which makes us believe in the immediacy of events and our consciousness of them.

In her discussion of this paper, Katy Bogliatto suggests that the interval of 0.5 seconds that in reality exists might contain unsymbolised sensory traces which would "add up" throughout life and function as an "underground spring". It's tempting to draw an analogy between the "unconscious compression of time" and the Freudian unconscious, by definition not capable of consciousness. Perhaps the shared roots of the reductionist school of Helmoltz invites such parallel (Bernfeld, 1944). As Freud continued to work with this framework throughout his life, we might think of these links as "Benini with Freud".

And yet, while on one hand, Benini describes time as "the inborn scaffolding of brain mechanisms in which the whole reality, including that of mental life, is included", on the other, it must be recognised that knowledge of time from the perspective of cognitive neuroscience remains rather obscure due to the complexity of the mechanisms involved. Although highly plausible, the claim of time being "an innate scaffolding" is therefore open to question; a premise more than a conclusion – "as if" time were an innate scaffolding of the brain.

Physics: a stubborn illusion

Caution marks both the approach that scientists take to their experiment and the conclusions drawn. G. Münster's text, in its extreme condensation, is an exemplar of the clarity that can arise from the scientific attitude. The process of reduction and simplification of issues has led to decisive advances in physics. Take the question of time – physicists define it according to the problem at hand. Einstein, half jokingly, defined time as what is measured by a clock. There is no subjectivity; gone too is the 'now' as physics concerns itself with universal laws that stand all of time.

In contrast, the *nature* of time is a question for philosophers; but Münster adds they don't reach agreement amongst themselves even when they don't find it a nonsensical question. He reminds us that with McTaggart, we can even propose more than one definition of time, or rather, more than one way of thinking about the unfolding of time. For the philosophers of series A, time can be divided into past, present and future, while for those of series B, time is linear with an earlier or later equation. The physicist Münster regards these as metaphysical questions. Even worse, the time that physics works with is not that of physiology, psychology or sociology.

Amidst this thicket of views, Münster comes to our rescue in saying that after all, the opposition between the two perceptions of time – linear and punctuated – is only different ways of representing reality. In offering this subjective agreement on the signification of clocks, he takes up what is known as 'a position of convention' in the philosophy of science.

The time of clocks is set with periodic processes, the measurement of which uses a specific method called 'operational'. The young Münster, still in the common psychology of life (the one we think with most of the time), might wonder how the atomic clock is regarded as the most accurate if there's no more accurate clock to measure it against.

Further, in physics, the concept of time can only be understood within a framework used for describing nature. It is 'theory laden'; its meaning can only be understood within a system that incorporates it – a parameter referred to as 't'. This theoretical parameter derives its significance from the framework of a theoretical description of a specific domain of phenomena. It's a tight framing!

While we begin with an expectation that science will tell us about the world clearly and completely, we are disappointed when we discover that we have been holding a false idea of science, a crude empiricism. In its place, we are confronted with the realisation that the scientific approach destroys our expectations of a clear, precise and universal definition. It offers us this instead: "Time is an idealised concept, which is tied to the phenomena and experiments by means of models, idealisations and bridge principles."

In fields such as psychology, thermodynamics and even cosmology, the irreversible nature of processes is key to understanding the concept of time and its flow – "the arrow of time". Physics is more circumspect and takes the stance of 'semantic consistency' or agreed interpretation given that the arrow of time lacks a unified explanation. This agreement acts as a conventional rule: while it doesn't negate the truth of the concept, it indicates that its validity cannot be (or hasn't yet been) definitely proven.[3]

Physics has the most to say about time through the theory of relativity – a clock in motion ticks more slowly than one at rest, and this effect has to do with the difference in speed between the clock and the observer. This principle of relativity applies not only to clocks but to all objects, including living organisms. Prior to Einstein, the notions of simultaneity, an absolute time and a 'now' that was the same for everyone, were unquestioned assumptions. The theory of relativity points out the ambiguous quality of simultaneity, taking into factor the speed at which we move and the distance between the two locations of the 'now'. Therefore, there is no way of knowing whether a scientific experiment carried out elsewhere (say, in a different location or at a different velocity relative to you) is done or not yet done. More precisely, and here the words are particularly important: "there is no way of giving meaning to the assertion of the 'complete or open' status" (of the experiment). Münster considers the conundrum of not being able to make sense of an assertion "the most serious problem in the philosophy of time."

Hence, he reminds us that Einstein, "a determinist", famously wrote of his difficulty as a *believing* scientist: "The distinction between past, present and future only has the meaning of an illusion, though a stubborn one." Which conception of scientific knowledge one works with and how one obtains it are therefore primary. The big questions of Being cannot be tackled; instead, we proceed through reduction and simplification. Charlotta Björklind reflected in her in-depth commentary: "We must be careful to not speculate too much about manifest similarities"; analogies are "necessarily metaphorical and a rough description." As Münster demonstrates, we are faced with the limitations of the tools we employ, the boundaries of our understanding and our models of representation.

While the richness of these perspectives may have evocative – or perhaps only analogical – power, we return to the challenge of identifying where the sciences (especially the hard sciences) intersect with psychoanalysis. The physicists' insistence on strictly defining time in relation to the specific problem at hand should give us food for thought. Psychoanalysts may feel closer to the notion that the modalities of the experiment modify what is being observed or how the devices intrinsic to the modality of the session influence what emerges.

Clinic and its impact

The clinical material presented with great generosity by Bernd Nissen and discussed in depth by Jasminka Šuljagić had a strong effect on the symposium's proceedings at the present time of the exchange. We struggled to turn away from it; we kept returning, needing to talk about it again and again. We might account for it by recognising that the clinical material had a somewhat traumatic effect on the audience and also perhaps on the presenter, since he had already presented it previously. On a purely descriptive level, the intensity of the listeners' experience 'didn't go away'; it couldn't be forgotten. From another point of view, the clinical narrative was so compelling that we found it hard not to try and 'explain' it, to make it less wild and disturbing. Here, 'explain' means to make it intelligible, to 'familiarise' it. The intensity of its destructive force and the struggle to elaborate it also account for the impact of this clinical material.

Nissen's text demarcates two distinct currents in psychoanalysis. The first is the line of thought that follows Strachey's comment that the concept of *après-coup* proposed by Freud in his theory of seduction is a 'superseded' theory (Freud, 1900). The English translation as 'deferred action' suggests that discharge takes place at a later stage. This would be more in line with the theory of abreaction, and Freud himself effectively "superseded" the idea of therapy being a process of discharging retained (or 'un-experienced'?) emotional charge.

The second current, predominant in France, believes that the mechanism of *après-coup* permeates all of Freud's work and is central, since it resignifies the history, modifying the meaning of the first occurrence. *Après-coup* is, strictly speaking, an action on a 'representation', another major concept. Freud's distinction between representation, *Vorstellung*, and presentation, *Darstellung* (the way in which things manifest themselves), offers profound coherence.[4]

In his elaboration, Nissen does not seem to differentiate between representation and presentation, as a result of which the notions of psychic apparatus and mnesic trace lose their importance. The hypothesis of the unconscious as 'atemporal' then seems untenable.

We offer two further comments: one on the interval, the other on the *zeitlos*.

On the one hand, the notions of representation and psychic apparatus enable psychoanalysis to escape from a phenomenology of the immediate; they presuppose a processing of the stimulus and a long circuit that nevertheless gives the impression of direct access. Both Benini and Münster, each in his own way, insist on something analogous: the former with the enigma of the interval, the latter with the fact that my 'now' is not really someone else's 'now'.

On the other hand, in Freud's *zeitlos* unconscious, "without time" denotes not temporally ordered but various times being all mixed up. Here, an experience or event quite "early" is still alive with all its intensity and consequences. This crucial point links *zeitlos* with the therapeutic effect of psychoanalysis: "the unalterability by time of the repressed," as Freud suggests, implies that unconscious effects are permanent as long as they "are not made conscious by the work of analysis." Only when made conscious do they enter 'history'. Freud (1933) adds that "it is on this that the therapeutic effect of analytic treatment rests to no small extent."

Of course, the unconscious is a hypothesis, even if Freud had considered that to become an analyst, conviction – even belief! – in the existence of the unconscious was necessary from undergoing one's own analysis. Even so, the savagery of the unconscious can be forgotten, and we might slide into thinking of it as something mild, as if it were the non-conscious rather than something that Freud described as remaining unknowable in itself. There is also the risk that psychoanalytic notions lose the force of their strangeness and challenging quality through familiarisation. Freud's second hypothesis of the mind shocks and disturbs us once more, reminding us that we are dealing with something we are always trying to grasp, and there is no possibility of settling on a clear, defined and steady position.

There is also the danger, be it with the unconscious or the second drive theory, that reification (commodification) can set in, transforming a hypothesis into a 'thing'. Yet in our clinical work, we daily deal with "things' rather concrete even if not 'real' in the usual sense of the word, perhaps requiring reification in the clinic and non-reification in theory. At the same time, there is the risk that psychoanalysts sometimes allow themselves to be persuaded by epistemological currents which can seem a caricature of science.

The question of theory

Jorge Canestri's text is, first and foremost, a warning about the pitfalls of a dialogue between neuroscience and psychoanalysis and perhaps even a warning about the idea we have regarding the status of psychoanalysis.

There are three caveats to be kept in mind at the outset. The first is that since we cannot know all the determinants of a present situation, prediction is unreliable. Secondly, that ideology plays an important role in the choices we make. Finally, the need to reconsider the belief that we can do without theory, or even that we do without theory; this is the desire to rely on data and observation without an overall theoretical reflection. Canestri reminds us of Niels Bohr's observation that in interpreting the information that physics obtains from the outside world, the researcher imposes his own code of symbols.

Theories are built from background or historical knowledge and the knowledge of the time, crafted together with the theorist's choices. The theorist's work is hence largely a work of imagination. Canestri distinguishes between theoretical models which correspond to the object in a fairly complete way and imaginary models which have above all a heuristic value, i.e. for research and discovery. In other words, the proliferation of models and theories in psychoanalysis is not a handicap but rather indicates the need for new models to enrich our discipline. Canestri thinks new comparisons and analogies are always needed since no single one is an exact or complete "fit' (Canestri, 2018).

In the background stands the ontological question of the status of the psychic – Freud returned to this throughout his work, even as we continue to ponder the link between the body and the mental (or psychic). Canestri writes that when dealing with human beings, biology is always evident at the basic level. But drawing on a classification proposed by Donald Davidson, he goes on to say that while Freud's materialism (and hopefully our own) implies an identity between the two, body and mind, from an epistemological point of view, we have to admit a descriptive, methodological and conceptual dualism. In other words, psychoanalysis can loudly assert its own way of investigating, theorising and use of its conceptual apparatus. He recalls Noam Chomsky's admission that while linguistics has biological underpinnings, he believes linguistics to have its own rights. We might add that it is precisely because Chomsky begins by situating himself on a clearly materialistic plane that he is then able to develop theories for the analysis of language and discourse.

We previously highlighted the need to pay attention to the analogies offered to us by the language of different disciplines. Davidson, Canestri reminds us, believes that the problem of interpretation is already present between two speakers of the same language; that translation operates in different uses of the same language – an idea very present in psychoanalysis. Approaching this theme from another angle, we can recall with Canestri that the data we work with presuppose the use of material and conceptual tools. As Münster and all serious epistemology have said, observation is loaded with theory. Canestri highlights: "The unity of analysis, from an epistemological point of view, is theory."

The unbridgeable

Hartog's text performs the crucial epistemological task of elucidating the framework of thought on its own terms while firmly situating itself within its historical context. From the outset, he establishes his own epistemological perspective and, guided by the insights of Michel de Certeau and Jules Michelet, successfully distances himself from the triumphant structuralism that characterised the post–World War II era. His interrogation of his own path resonates with an analyst's ear, especially as he addresses Ulysses and describes "his sudden awareness of an unbridgeable divide between two selves." There are words and categories that do not yet belong to Ulysses; at the same time, there is a past that is both his and no longer his. It brings to mind Hartog's beautiful phrase in relation to impossible simultaneity: "One might say that at the time (of the Berlin wall), East Berliners and West Berliners were and were not contemporaries."

The proximity of a historian's approach to psychoanalysis is hardly surprising. And Hartog's text particularly fulfils the aspiration of the symposium to hear about the state of research in other fields into the subject of time, and beyond that, to hear about the foundation on which they base their studies. An example of how Hartog achieves this twin objective with great clarity is his description of Reinhart Koselleck's two parameters – the space of experience and the horizon of expectation – as "metacategories". Hence Joëlle Picard's acknowledgement of him as a metahistorian, in the vein of Freud's metapsychology.[5]

Two further links between history and psychoanalysis are worth highlighting. The first consideration is that our way of perceiving temporality is a given since we are part of a culture whose presuppositions we live by as realities in themselves. However, as psychoanalysts, our task involves questioning the nature of cultural 'facts' – matters which in being named 'obvious' have been collectively accepted unthinkingly. Related is the axis of the historian's search for implicit cultural underpinnings to data and their textual narrative, which parallels our analytic listening for unconscious elements underlying the discourse of our patients.

We might do well to take note that Hartog's complete text operates on a time lag, and we have the 'young' Hartog here from 1968 just as we had the young Münster wondering about atomic time. What's more, the text is entirely constructed in terms of 'encounters'. While we had particularly solicited this personal dimension with our invitation, does it invalidate his theorizing? Münster inquired this of himself too.

Our last words, perhaps aptly, are to acknowledge the presence of great works of literature which have featured in many of the papers. These have ranged from Borges to Thomas Mann via Appelfeld and the grandeur of one of the first literary creations of the Western world – *The Odyssey*.

Note

1 It's necessary to remind that Strachey translated *Vorstellung* by idea and not by representation.
2 It's the penultimate note, written on August 22, 1939. Freud died on September 23, one month later.
3 Quantum physics has finally accepted that it cannot "lay its hands on Being", writes François Ladieu (2024) in a text published after our Symposium.
4 See Mark Solms' remarks on the use of *Nachträglichkeit* in the *Revised Standard Edition*, Mark Solms (2018) And also: Thomä, H., and N. Cheshire (1991).

5 In a 2024 lecture to the Belgian Society, Joëlle Picard returned at length to Hartog's question of simultaneity and non-simultaneity.

References

Bernfeld, S. (1944). Freud's earliest theories and the School of Helmholtz. *Psychoanalytic Quarterly* 13, 341–362

Canestri, J. (2018). Quelques idées sur la diversité des théories psychanalytiques et sur une perspective d'évolution pour la psychanalyse: un commentaire. *Revue française de psychanalyse* 82(3), 740–750

Freud, S. (1900). *SE* IV, *The Interpretation of Dreams*, p. 205 n 1.

Freud, S. (1920). *Beyond the Pleasure Principle*, OCP XV, p. 299, SE XVIII, 28, GW XIII 27–28.

Freud, S. (1933). *New Introductory Lectures on Psycho-Analysis*, lecture XXXI, SE XXII, p. 74; *OCP*, XIX, 157 *GW* XV, 80–81.

Freud, S. (1940). *Findings, Ideas, problems*, OCP XX, 320, GW XVII, 152. SE XXIII, p. 300.

Ladieu, F. (2024). « La Physique: une science exacte où règne l'indétermination », *Revue française de psychanlayse* 88(2), 37–47, 45.

Picard, J. (2024). François Hartog: régimes d'historicité et métahistoire. Quels intérêts pour l'analyste ? Unpublished.

Solms, M. (2018). Extracts from the Revised Standard Edition of Freud's Page 29. Complete psychological works. *The International Journal of Psychoanalysis* 99(1), 11–57. https://doi.org/10.1080/00207578.2017.1408306

Thomä, H., & Cheshire, N. (1991). Freud's Nachträglichkeit and Strachey's 'Deferred Action': Trauma, constructions and the direction of causality. *International Review of Psycho-Analysis* 18, 407–428

Index

Note: Page numbers in *italics* indicate a figure on the corresponding page.

For Product Safety Concerns and Information please contact our EU
representative GPSR@taylorandfrancis.com
Taylor & Francis Verlag GmbH, Kaufingerstraße 24, 80331 München, Germany

www.ingramcontent.com/pod-product-compliance
Lightning Source LLC
Chambersburg PA
CBHW050614280326
41932CB00016B/3036

9 781041 114055